Keys to Help You Unlock the Bible

Keys to Help You Unlock the Bible

A Metaphysical Interpretation

Tim Carpenter

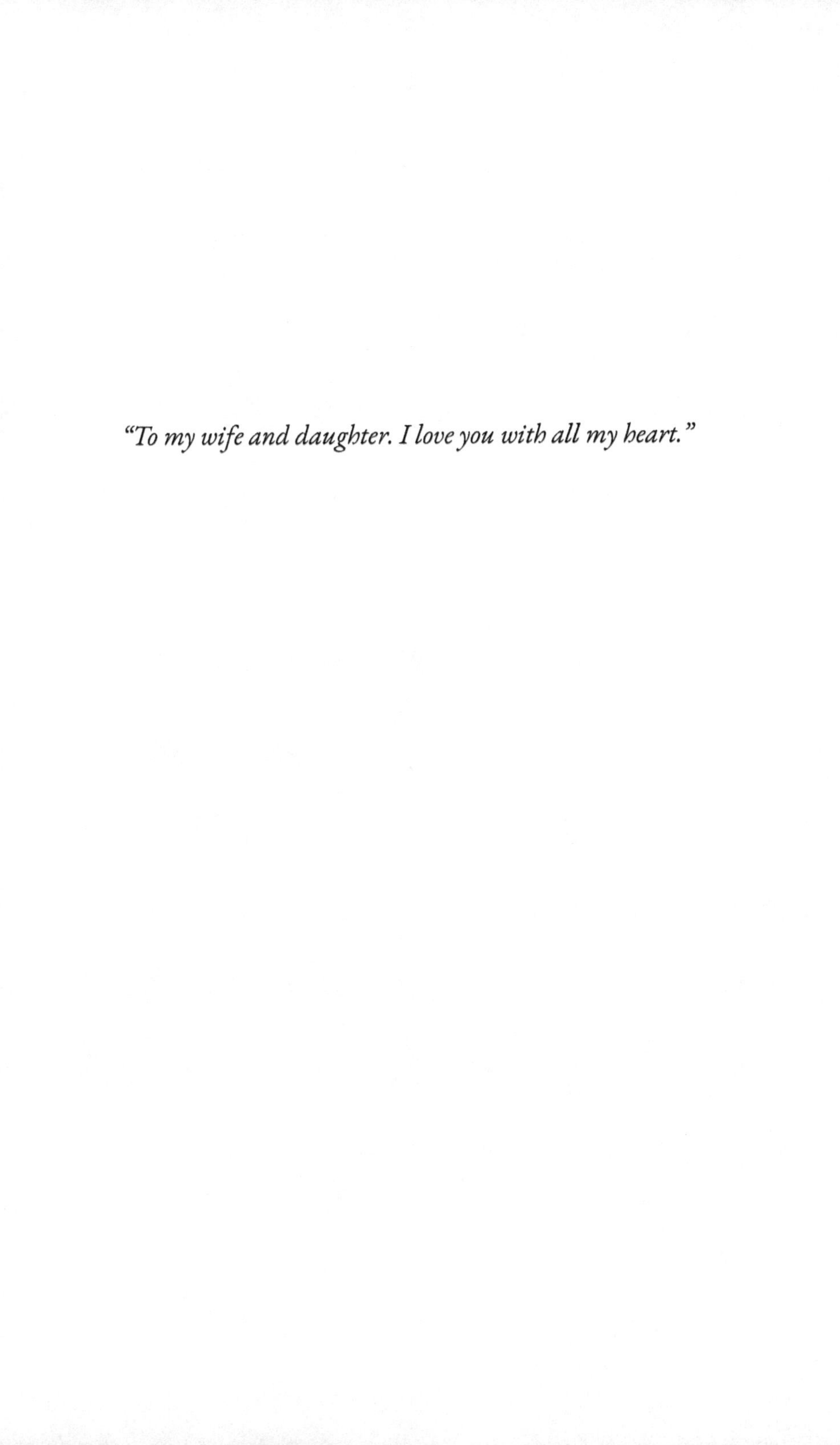

"To my wife and daughter. I love you with all my heart."

Creationism Vs Evolution

Science and religion, two seemingly opposite belief systems, are actually two sides of the same pole. One focuses on the outer world, the tangible and physical realm of matter, while the other delves into the inner world of psyche, soul, and spirit. Science seeks to understand how the material universe functions and what it is composed of, while religion explores the deeper questions of why the universe exists and what purpose each thing holds. Together, they form a harmonious partnership that complements and enriches one another.

As we continue to explore the mysteries of consciousness, a topic that has captivated religious scholars for centuries, science and religion are finally beginning to merge. In fact, some believe that the Bible may be the most advanced scientific book ever written. As we progress further in our understanding of consciousness, it is not hard to imagine a future where scientists and priests are one and the same.

For instance, let's consider the power of sound and language. During a conversation, I sit before you, my mind filled with intangible thoughts. Yet, through invisible forces, I am able to project these thoughts by manipulating air with my mouth, tongue, and lips to create sound waves. These invisible waves travel through space until they reach your ears. The intricate anatomy of your ear picks up these vibrations and sends them to your brain via electrical signals. And somehow, through this complex process involving invisible forces and intangible concepts, my thoughts have now become tangible in your mind as well.

In essence, we are all unique expressions of an infinite lattice of information that permeates the entire universe. We experience life through the lens of our individual biotechnology, shaping our understanding of reality. And it is through science and religion that we continue to unravel the mysteries of existence and our place within it.

This would not be possible if 'my' consciousness and 'your' consciousness were separate, as we would have no unifying substance through which to exchange these intangible ideas. It is possible if we understand that there is one substance, which is pure intelligence itself, and we all partake of it.

Deep in the endless debate between science and religion lies a hidden truth, one that must be addressed in order to move beyond the constant bickering. It is the elephant in the room - the book of Genesis and its creation story. For centuries, it has been misinterpreted and misunderstood, with most people unaware that there are actually two distinct versions of creation within its pages. The first, found in chapter one, depicts God, referred to as Elohim, creating an idealized version of the universe. The second, found in chapter two, shows God manifested as Jehovah bringing these ideals into existence.

Religion, especially through the bible, focuses on the evolution of the human soul and our relationship with God. It serves as a guidebook for humanity's journey towards becoming the ideal version of ourselves, living in unity with all that exists. It acknowledges our inevitable fall into materialism and separation but ultimately aims for our return to unity with the whole, merging both the material and ideal realms.

One common misconception is that the theory of evolution and the story of Genesis are incompatible - that belief in one means rejecting the other. However, this is not true; even Charles Darwin, the originator of evolution himself, believed in God as the first cause. This notion can be traced back to Albert Einstein's words: "A human being is a part of the whole, called by us 'Universe,' a part limited in time and space. He experiences himself, his thoughts and his feelings as something separate from the rest - a kind of optical delusion of his consciousness. The striving to free oneself from this delusion is the one issue of true religion. Not to nourish it but to try to overcome it is the way to reach the attainable measure of peace of mind." By understanding this interconnectedness between science and religion, we can break free from narrow-minded thinking and open ourselves up to new perspectives and possibilities. In Christianity, Jesus Christ taught that God is not a physical being, but rather a spirit that can only be worshipped through one's own spirit and in truth (John 4:24). This emphasizes the idea that our true connection to God is through our consciousness. Or if we were to use the original Greek word it would be psyche, which in Greek means, breath and soul. So, our psyche, the totality of our consciousness is our soul.

What exactly is this higher power that we are connected to? In Christianity, this higher power is known as Jehovah or Yaweh, which means I AM that I AM, pure unconditioned awareness of being.

But who is Jehovah? According to Christian belief, Jehovah is the infinite intelligence and divine mind that ideates and creates the universe. As it says in John 1:1-3, "In the beginning was the Word, and the Word was with God, and the Word was God. He was with God in the beginning. Through him all things were made; without him nothing was made that has been made."

The word logos in Greek can be translated as wisdom or principle of divine reason and creative order. This divine wisdom and creative power is brought forth into manifestation through Christ, who is known as the prism of God.

Just as our thoughts shape our reality on a personal level, this divine mind shapes the entire universe according to a specific sequence and process of condensation. This process can be seen in nature as well – from a seed growing into a tree to an embryo developing into a human being. All of these processes follow a specific sequence of growth guided by divine intelligence.

This principle of divine reason and creative order also applies to human beings. We are created in God's image and have been given the power to manifest our thoughts into reality. This power comes from our connection to the infinite intelligence of God.

Jesus Christ emphasized this truth when he said in Mark 11:24, "Therefore I tell you, whatever you ask for in prayer, believe that you have received it, and it will be yours." This shows us that our thoughts and beliefs have creative power to shape our reality according to divine order.

In the beginning, God's word spoke creation into existence. He carefully crafted each stage of development, from the formation of stars to the emergence of life on Earth.

This parallels with scientific theories like the Big Bang, which suggest a gradual process of evolution over billions of years. However, beyond debates about the origins of our universe, one truth remains: there is a profound connection between our consciousness and the act of creation.

As we align ourselves with God's divine consciousness, we tap into a greater understanding of ourselves and our purpose in this vast universe. We realize that we are not isolated beings, but interconnected threads woven into the grand tapestry of God's design. "For by him all things were created...and in him all things hold together" (Colossians 1:16-17). Let us embrace this interconnectedness and let our creations reflect the beauty and love of our Creator.

The epiphany of this truth can bring about a profound sense of inner tranquility and oneness with both ourselves and those around us. It opens the door for us to tap into the infinite power of divine consciousness to manifest our deepest desires and catalyze positive change in our lives.

In Hebrew, words are complex and multi-layered, often carrying a variety of meanings depending on the context in which they are used. They also have a gender assigned to them, either feminine or masculine. For example, the word for light in Hebrew is "ohr." In Genesis 1:3, when Elohim declares "let there be ohr," it is not referring to physical light like that of the sun, but rather an energetic substance that brings order to chaos. This aligns with Jesus' statement in John 8:12, "I Am the light of the world. Whoever follows me will never walk in darkness but will have the light of life." Combined with John 1:1, where it is stated that "in the beginning was the Word (logos) and the Word (logos) was with God and was God," we can see that Christ is the prism through which the chaotic universe becomes unified in harmony and order. However, Jesus also bestows this same light onto us in Matthew 5:14 when he proclaims, "you are the light of the world."

What then, is the medium through which all things are perceived and understood? What allows us to feel and experience the world around us on both an individual and collective level? Consciousness. Throughout biblical texts, consciousness is referred to as light and equated with life. With this understanding, we can now delve into Genesis with a deeper level of comprehension. This may be a challenging journey at first, but it is necessary to grasp these concepts before moving forward in our exploration of this book.

Introduction To The Study Of Genesis

A way to look at Genesis is as a meditation. Genesis Chapter 1 can be seen as a meditation that helps establish order and harmony within the consciousness. This is the work of God known as Elohim, universal mind bringing a greater expanse of life and harmony through principle and ideal. The 2nd chapter of Genesis can be seen as the impartation of this newly established order within consciousness, and how it unfolds through our soul into our lives here on earth. This is the work of God known as Jehovah in chapter 2, to take the impersonal ideals and make them personal through the formation of Adam and Eve. As the principles and ideals of Elohim are brought forth through our relation with Jehovah we gradually gain more and more understanding and this is shown through more and more detail being added through the stages of creation. We can see it as spiritual groundwork, the laying down of principles and then the product of taking action on those principles, which leads all who awaken to this process to the greatest and fullest experience of life, complete conscious union with God. Which is Christ consciousness. Once Christ the quickening spirit is within us we are to let the same mind that is in Christ Jesus be also in us, to have the mind of Christ. Apostle Paul also says that that Jesus thought it not robbery to be equal with God. This sounds like a great thing, but when we realize that God is pure bestowal, meaning there is no selfish desire in him, he is all giving all the time, making ourselves equal with God means that we must pour out everything that would build itself up in opposition to the natural flow and evolution of life. Everything your personality has worked so hard to build, develop and cling on to must be burned away in the light of the truth that in reality, all belongs to God. The man Jesus is our perfect example, as he loved his life, the life of Jesus the man from Nazareth, not, even unto death. This is because to live from Christ consciousness is to know that all things are intrinsically connected there is no mine, and your consciousness, there is only God. It's to live from the revelation that we are not living life, but life is living us. If the idea Christ consciousness sounds a bit new agey, and weird, it really isn't that difficult to grasp. The internet is the same idea just made through a finite, limited understanding. Each server or host transmits data through optical cables to a cell tower which then transmits the information through electromagnetic waves that are decoded and digitized into what you see on your device. The same is true of Christ Consciousness. All the information that ever was, is, or will be, is fully present here and now and through the bio-computer which is our body we're constantly filtering and decoding this information into what we perceive as our current reality. The internet is the manifestation of the fallen hive mind of humanity. But instead of content generated from people then coded and digitized through our devices we align ourselves with ancient and infinite universal life principals and become channels through which this divine information becomes manifest upon the earth. In effect perpetuating the kingdom of heaven on earth. The grand overarching purpose of Genesis is to establish within ourselves a concrete landscape of these universal life principals by meditating on the order and process of how God creates and brings all things into being, by doing this we build a stable foundation for our soul body to grow from. So with this said let's start building this understanding within us.

GENESIS CHAPTER 1

Genesis 1:1 In the beginning, God created the heavens and the earth. 2 The earth was without form, and void; and darkness was on the face of the deep. And the Spirit of God was hovering over the face of the waters. 3 Then God said, "Let there be light"; and there was light. 4 And God saw the light, that it was good; and God divided the light from the darkness. 5 God called the light Day, and the darkness He called Night. So, the evening and the morning were the first day.

In the first chapter of Genesis, we are introduced to the name of God - Elohim. This name is composed of four Hebrew letters: Aleph, Lamed, Hey, and Mem, which each hold significant meaning. Aleph represents strength and leadership, Lamed represents authority and guidance, Hey represents revelation and communication, and Mem represents water. So, when we read "in the beginning Elohim created the heavens and the earth," we can understand it as "God, the strong leader who speaks with authority gives revelation through mighty work that separates the waters." In John 4:24, Jesus tells us that "God is spirit," emphasizing the all-encompassing nature of God. And if God is within us, then we must look inward to find Him.

Jesus goes on to tell us that "the kingdom of heaven is within us," which means that our spiritual consciousness is the most subtle and internal aspect of ourselves, while our material existence is outer and less important. This concept ties in with the creation story in Genesis - the active force of spirit creating and shaping the passive matter of earth. However, it's important to note that at this point in the story, earth is formless and void - not yet a fully formed material world.

The mention of water in this passage also holds significance. In biblical symbolism, water often represents unseen potential or the psychic realm. It is through this subtle substance that spiritual consciousness filters into distinct identities. In his conversation with Nicodemus (John 3:5), Jesus explains that one must be "born of water and Spirit" to enter into the kingdom of God. This reaffirms the idea that our physical birth is just one small part of our journey towards spiritual enlightenment which is our rebirth.

In the gospel of John, it is written that "that which is born of the flesh is flesh; and that which is born of the Spirit is spirit" (John 3:5-6). In other words, unless one undergoes a psychological and spiritual transformation, they cannot leave behind their old self and be reborn anew. To fully understand this concept, let us examine the story of Jesus turning water into wine in John 2. The stone jars represent a material interpretation of scripture, which must then be intellectually and psychologically understood before it can be transformed into spiritual wisdom - represented by wine. This symbolism reflects Jesus' purpose on earth - to bring spiritual understanding to humanity and bridge the gap between heaven and earth.

Water, often used to symbolize the psychic realm, acts as a link between active spiritual energy and passive elemental substance. In

Genesis, it is said that "Elohim was hovering over the face of the waters," indicating that spiritual energy was moving upon the unmanifest potential of psychic substance. Elohim, representing God as spirit, uses the word or idea (logos) as a vehicle for creation. Just as a word contains infinite ideas within itself, logos serves as a prism through which God's infinite potentiality radiates. Everything has an underlying idea - chairs represent comfort, music represents harmony, and the internet represents global connection. This concept of involution (forming ideals) and evolution (unfolding those ideals) can also be seen in our daily lives, as we have ideas that are then carried out by our physical bodies.

In verse two of Genesis, when it speaks of the earth being formless and void, it refers to Elohim's idea or plan for the earth before any physical manifestation occurs. This ties in with the Hebrew word for light - ohr - meaning order. Through the word (logos), Elohim brings order to chaos and brings clarity to darkness (undeveloped capacities). The division of light and darkness also represents the separation of known and clear ideas (day) from unknown and undeveloped potentials (night).

DAY 2

6 Then God said, "Let there be a firmament in the midst of the waters, and let it divide the waters from the waters." 7 Thus God made the firmament and divided the waters which were under the firmament from the waters which were above the firmament, and it was so. 8 And God called the firmament Heaven. So the evening and the morning were the second day.

The firmament in the midst of the waters represents the barrier between the conscious and subconscious mind. Just as water can be a source of life, it can also be a destructive force - representing the potential for both positive and negative thoughts within our subconscious. The separation of these waters allows for the development and evolution of consciousness, as we are able to bring light and order to our subconscious through understanding and utilizing our conscious mind when we align them with heavenly principles.

Verse 8 states that God called the firmament Heaven. This symbolizes the connection between our innermost being (mind) and the divine consciousness above. By bringing harmony and balance to our conscious and subconscious minds, we align ourselves with the divine will represented by Heaven.

The second day of creation highlights the importance of mental discipline and harnessing our thoughts for positive growth and development. It is through this process that we are able to transform chaotic potential into harmonious manifestation - just as Elohim did by separating the waters.

This concept is also reflected in Jesus' teachings, particularly in Matthew 6:22-23 where he says, "The eye is the lamp of the body; so then if your eye is clear, your whole body will be full of light." This speaks to the power of controlling our thoughts and perceptions as they shape our reality.

In essence, stage two emphasizes the importance of creating a firmament or barrier between our conscious and subconscious minds - allowing us to separate potential from manifestation, chaos from order, and darkness from light. By doing so, we align ourselves with divine guidance and become co-creators in this ever-evolving universe.

Like the dawn breaking each morning, the mention of "morning" at the end of each stage signifies the unending and limitless nature of Elohim's work. Just as the sun rises each day, so does Elohim's work, which continues in an endless cycle of the evening to morning. This mirrors the concept of eternity and infinite potential found in passages such as Psalm 90:2, which states, "Before the mountains were born or you brought forth the whole world, from everlasting to everlasting you are God."

. . .

DAY 3

9 Then God said, "Let the waters under the heavens be gathered together into one place, and let the dry land appear," and it was so. 10 And God called the dry land Earth, and the gathering together of the waters He called Seas. And God saw that it was good.

11 Then God said, "Let the earth bring forth grass, the herb that yields seed, and the fruit tree that yields fruit according to its kind, whose seed is in itself, on the earth," and it was so. 12 And the earth brought forth grass, the herb that yields seed according to its kind, and the tree that yields fruit, whose seed is in itself according to its kind. And God saw that it was good. 13 So the evening and the morning were the third day.

DAY 4

14 Then God said, "Let there be lights in the firmament of the heavens to divide the day from the night; and let them be for signs and seasons, and for days and years; 15 and let them be for lights in the firmament of the heavens to give light on the earth"; and it was so. 16 Then God made two great lights: the greater light to rule the day, and the lesser light to rule the night. He made the stars also. 17 God set them in the firmament of the heavens to give light on the earth, 18 and to rule over the day and over the night, and to divide the light from the darkness. And God saw that it was good. 19 So the evening and the morning were the fourth day.

As we delve deeper into the stages of creation, we witness the magnificent power and wisdom of Elohim. In the beginning, He spoke and said, "Let there be light," and thus began the process of bringing order to chaos, of awakening consciousness. And now, in this fourth stage, we see His divine plan unfolding even further as

He commands, "Let there be lights in the firmament of the heavens to divide day from night." This firmament symbolizes the harmonious balance between higher and lower potentialities, between conscious and subconscious forces. It is a state of perfect harmony, referred to as Heaven.

But before this stage, it is written that "the evening and morning were 'this' day." This reminds us that time does not exist in the same way for Elohim as it does for us. For Him, everything is already planned and complete in His mind. These evenings and mornings represent phases of transition from pure potentiality to manifest reality. And now, with the creation of the sun and moon, we see an even greater division between day and night. Without these celestial bodies being in perfect balance, life on Earth would not be possible.

The sun, with its fiery rays, brings illumination and warmth during the day. And at night, when darkness falls, the moon reflects the light of the sun, providing a gentle glow to guide us through the night. Just like in all things in nature, there are masculine and feminine aspects at play here. The sun represents the active force, while the moon embodies passivity. Together, they create a beautiful dance of balance within the universal mind.

And it is this balance that allows for life to thrive on Earth. Without the revolution of the earth around the sun or the symphony of active and passive forces within us, organic life would not have a chance to grow and flourish. It is through this constant cycle of revolution and synchronization that all things are held in perfect balance, allowing for life to emerge and unfold along harmonious lines.

As we reflect on the creation story, we see how each stage builds upon the next. From the division of waters above and below by the firmament, we now witness the refining idea of complementing forces: the sun and moon. And from these higher and lower potentialities, all other things unfold along harmonious lines, following the rhythm of seasons, days, and years. Truly, Elohim's divine plan is a masterpiece of balance and harmony.

DAY 5

Then God said, "Let the waters abound with an abundance of living creatures, and let birds fly above the earth across the face of the firmament of the heavens." 21 So God created great sea creatures and every living thing that moves, with which the waters abounded, according to their kind, and every winged bird according to its kind. And God saw that it was good. 22 And God blessed them, saying, "Be fruitful and multiply, and fill the waters in the seas, and let birds multiply on the earth." 23 So the evening and the morning were the fifth day.

As the journey of involution continues, the fifth stage is marked by the emergence of sensations and differentiation, embodied by the creatures dwelling in the vast sea and soaring through the heavens. These beings are the manifestations of our own identities, sprouting from the fertile soil of our minds like seeds that bear fruit after their kind. Just as Jonah was swallowed by a great sea monster before finding enlightenment, these sea creatures represent unconscious thoughts that have yet to be illuminated by the light of understanding. They lurk in the depths, waiting to be discovered and tamed by our conscious awareness, just as the Lord calmed the raging sea with His word.

Unruly thoughts, like untamed beasts, lurk in the depths of our subconscious. They are the dark corners of our minds that we try to ignore, but they hold immense power over us if left unchecked. As Carl Jung warned, these thoughts can manifest as our "shadow self," wreaking havoc on our lives and relationships. But just as birds of the air soar through the vast expanse of the heavens, some thoughts have the potential to connect us with spiritual truths beyond our earthly realm. Like the creation story in Genesis, where darkness first existed before light emerged, these thoughts, too, must be acknowledged and integrated into our consciousness in order for us to find balance and peace in our lives. So let us not fear the shadow but embrace it with understanding and wisdom, for it is a part of our human experience and necessary for our growth.

DAY 6

24 Then God said, "Let the earth bring forth the living creature according to its kind: cattle and creeping thing and beast of the earth, each according to its kind," and it was so. 25 And God made the beast of the earth according to its kind, cattle according to its kind, and everything that creeps on the earth according to its kind. And God saw that it was good.

26 Then God said, "Let Us make man in Our image, according to Our likeness; let them have dominion over the fish of the sea, over the birds of the air, and over the cattle, over all the earth and over every creeping thing that creeps on the earth." 27 So God created man in His own image; in the image of God He created him; male and female He created them. 28 Then God blessed them, and God said to them, "Be fruitful and multiply; fill the earth and subdue it; have dominion over the fish of the sea, over the birds of the air, and over every living thing that moves on the earth."

29 And God said, "See, I have given you every herb that yields seed which is on the face of all the earth, and every tree whose fruit yields seed; to you, it shall be for food. 30 Also, to every beast of the earth, to every bird of the air, and to everything that creeps on the earth, in which there is life, I have given every green herb for food"; and it was so. 31 Then God saw everything that He had made, and indeed it was very good. So the evening and the morning were the sixth day.

In the sixth stage, we witness the manifestation of identities and ideas in the subtle psychic realms becoming more solidified with the emergence of cattle, creeping things, and beasts of the earth. No longer are these forces limited to the unconscious or confined to the sea and heavens; now, soul sensation plays a significant role in their existence. The universe is composed of three levels: spiritual, psychological, and material. We have traced the process of Elohim setting forth spiritual ideals that are then filtered and refined through the psychic realm before condensing into tangible sensations. Matter itself holds no life force; it is only through the infusion of spiritual energy from God-Mind that it becomes animated. Similar to an architect who envisions a building and then rationally plans its structure using universal laws like mathematics, Elohim shapes the universe according to divine inspiration. This is because humanity serves as a microcosm of the macrocosm. What Elohim does in the universal mind, we do individually, which will be further explained in the next step. With these modes of soul sensation now active and alive, Elohim turns his attention towards crystallizing all the forces of the "earth" into a human form, creating us in his image and likeness. It is important to note that when it says we are created in the image and likeness of God, this does not refer to our physical appearance since the material world has yet to fully take shape. Furthermore, it does not say we are created as the image and likeness but rather within or inside of it - within the imagination and likeness of Elohim, the pure divine mind.

The vast expanse of material existence is but a reflection of divine intelligence, a manifestation of ethereal energies transmuted into physical form through the alchemy of spiritual inspiration. Remember, dear reader, that the observer and the observed are one, intertwined in a dance of consciousness. For we are, at our core, meaning-making beings - each a microcosm of the ultimate reality - imbued with the very essence of God. Without this divine spark, life would be void of purpose and devoid of significance. Yet, through the lens of our own perceptions and awareness, we assign meaning to all things - from the lowly floor to the blazing fire, each existing in relation to one another within our minds. As we climb the mountain of consciousness, rising above the ego and delving deeper into the oneness of being, our vision becomes clearer and more encompassing. And so, just as a mountain symbolizes spiritual ascent in biblical texts, it also represents our journey towards a higher state of consciousness - where all is unified and illuminated by divinity.

In chapter two of Genesis, Elohim is referred to as Jehovah - or "I Am." This alludes to the idea that within God exists both male and female energies. After all, it is through Jehovah that Adam's rib is used to create Eve - symbolizing the duality within the divine unity. And so we see that even in creation, there is balance and harmony between these fundamental principles. For as Jehovah brings forth manifestations through denser modes of evolution, it serves as a reminder that both male and female exist within us all.

Thus concludes the sixth stage - a time of spiritual ignorance followed by illumination. And as we continue on our journey towards enlightenment, may we remember that God is not limited by human constructs or labels but rather encompasses all dualities within the divine whole

The vast expanse of material existence is but a reflection of divine intelligence, a manifestation of ethereal energies transmuted into physical form through the alchemy of spiritual inspiration. Remember, dear reader, that the observer and the observed are one, intertwined in a dance of consciousness. For we are, at our core, meaning-making beings - each a microcosm of the ultimate reality - imbued with the very essence of God. Without this divine spark, life would be void of purpose and devoid of significance. Yet, through the lens of our own perceptions and awareness, we assign meaning to all things - from the lowly floor to the blazing fire, each existing in relation to one another within our minds. As we climb the mountain of consciousness, rising above the ego and delving deeper into the oneness of being, our vision becomes clearer and more encompassing. And so, just as a mountain symbolizes spiritual ascent in biblical texts, it also represents our journey towards a higher state of consciousness - where all is unified and illuminated by divinity.

In chapter two of Genesis, Elohim is referred to as Jehovah - or "I Am." This alludes to the idea that within God exists both male and female energies. After all, it is through Jehovah that Adam's rib is used to create Eve - symbolizing the duality within the divine unity. And so we see that even in creation, there is balance and harmony between these fundamental principles. For as Jehovah brings forth manifestations through denser modes of evolution, it serves as a reminder that both male and female exist within us all.

Thus concludes the sixth stage - a time of spiritual ignorance followed by illumination. And as we continue on our journey towards enlightenment, may we remember that God is not limited by human constructs or labels but rather encompasses all dualities within the divine whole

GENESIS CHAPTER 2

2 Thus the heavens and the earth, and all the host of them, were finished. 2 And on the seventh day God ended His work which He had done, and He rested on the seventh day from all His work which He had done. 3 Then God blessed the seventh day and sanctified it because in it He rested from all His work which God had created and made.

Then, on the eighth day, God created Hell...just kidding! God is the roaring silence, the electric stillness that pulsates through all of creation. In Psalm 46:10, we are commanded to "be still and know" that He is God. Everything that has ever existed or will exist is contained in this present moment, fully alive and complete. Our thoughts are the vehicles through which we experience the absolute truth, but it is the eternal now that truly holds all things. The past is merely a collection of memories that we choose to feed into our present, and the future only exists in our imagination until it becomes our reality through conscious manifestation. We are forever existing in the present, and thus Elohim rests. This is why the seventh day is holy - because it symbolizes our recognition that everything is whole and complete in this very moment. And as for

Hell - let us put an end to the misconception that a loving God would create such a place.

Instead, let us understand that in the eyes of God, Heaven and Hell are one and the same - a state of being completely enveloped in His presence, either in a purified state free from all guilt, shame, and remorse through the blood of Christ or engulfed in terror and pain as His all-penetrating knowledge exposes every evil deed we have tried to hide. This was the original belief of Hell according to the early church and its saints. However, in medieval times, this concept evolved into a place of eternal torment for the pleasure of God, perpetuated by a church seeking to profit off of people's fear. As Psalm 139:8 reminds us, there is no escape from His ever-watchful presence, even in the depths of Hell.

God, the omnipotent and all-knowing, exists everywhere at once. There is not a single crevice or cavern hidden beneath the earth's surface that can contain Him. The concept of Hell as a literal fiery pit with demons torturing sinners was mainly created during the Medieval times and used as a fear tactic to motivate people to go fight in the crusades. Sadly, humans are often more motivated by fear than love. But let us not simply take my word for it; let us turn to the teachings of Church fathers, Saints, and great mystics such as St. Issac the Syrian who wrote about Gehenna (Hell) in his book Ascetical Homilies. He believed that those who go to Hell will be scourged not by fire and brimstone but by the intense agony of realizing their sins against love. This sorrow and regret will be sharper and more tormenting than any physical punishment.

According to Colossians 1:20, it is through God that all things can be reconciled to Him, whether on earth or in heaven. This act of reconciliation brings about peace, made possible by the shedding of blood on the cross. This reflects God's ultimate desire for all beings to be saved and reunited with Him. The concept of death and hell, then, cannot possibly be eternal as they go against the very principles of harmony and growth that characterize life. Thus, even in a fallen state, all things will ultimately be redeemed and brought back into alignment with God's will. It is a beautiful promise of restoration and salvation for all creation.

Peter Kreeft writes in his book – Everything You Ever Wanted to Know about Heaven – But Never Dreamed of Asking, "In reality, the damned are in the same place as the saved—in reality! But they hate it; it is their Hell. The saved love it, and it is their Heaven. It is like two people sitting side by side at an opera or a rock concert: the very thing that is Heaven to one is Hell to the other. Dostoyevski says, 'We are all in paradise, but we won't see it'...Hell is not literally the 'wrath of God.' The love of God is an objective fact; the 'wrath of God' is a human projection of our own wrath upon God, as Lady Julian saw—a disastrous misinterpretation of God's love as wrath. God really says to all His creatures, 'I know you, and I love you,' but they hear Him saying, 'I never knew you; depart from me.' It is like angry children misinterpreting their loving parents' affectionate advances as threats. They project their own hate onto their parents' love and experience love as an enemy—which it is: an enemy to their egotistic defenses against joy...

Pope Benedict XVI writes, "With death, our life choice becomes definitive—our life stands before the judge. Our choice, which in the course of an entire life takes on a certain shape, can have a variety of forms. There can be people who have totally destroyed their desire for truth and readiness to love, people for whom everything has become a lie, people who have lived for hatred and have suppressed all love within themselves. This is a terrifying thought, but alarming profiles of this type can be seen in certain figures of our own history. In such people, all would be beyond remedy, and the destruction of good would be irrevocable: this is what we mean by the word Hell." (Spe Salvi 45)

The great mystic Thomas Merton writes, "To worship our false selves is to worship nothing. And the worship of nothing is hell."

My thoughts could continue to pour out endlessly, but we must come to terms with the realization that the modern concept of hell as a separate place beneath us, where an angry God condemns evil and sinful people to eternal torment, stems from a dualistic belief system and is not in line with true Christianity. When the Bible declares that God is sovereign, omnipotent, omniscient, and omnipresent, we must take it at its word - meaning that there is no place where God is not present. This idea will be explored further in later chapters, but it is fitting to address it here at the end of Genesis 1 for obvious reasons.

Another common misconception about Christianity revolves around the question: "If indigenous tribespeople in remote parts of the world have never heard of Jesus, do they go to hell?" However, Christianity is not simply a label or a packaged belief system. It is not about conforming to a certain image or set of behaviors. Being a Christian means being a vessel for Christ, as stated in Galatians 2:20, "It is no longer I who live, but Christ lives in me." God, known as Elohim, is the formless absolute within which all things exist. On the other hand, Christ - also known as I Am and Jehovah - serves as the channel through which God reveals himself. And what does God reveal? Love.

Throughout his life, Jesus demonstrated this love endlessly. In Matthew 7:1 he says, "Do not judge, or you too will be judged." So if someone living in an isolated tribe deep in the rainforest lives their life with genuine, selfless love in their heart and does not condemn themselves or others, then yes - they will go to heaven. Because God is love and love belongs only to God. Love serves as the fundamental universal principle that gives everything its existence; it is the one unifying force that connects all beings. Therefore, anyone, regardless of their location or religious background, who aligns themselves with this love and lives in a way that embodies it, is already united with God and personifying Christ. They are true Christians, even if they have never heard the name of Jesus or stepped foot inside a church on Sunday. This is because Christ serves as the cosmic spectrum through which the light and love of God can be expressed and experienced.

In summary, 1 John 3:21 captures the essence of this section perfectly: "Beloved, if our heart does not condemn us, we have confidence before God."

Now that we have addressed these misconceptions, let us refocus on understanding the book of Genesis and where it leads us.

GENESIS CHAPTER 2:4

"These are the generations of the heavens and the earth when they were created, in the day that Jehovah made the earth and the heavens, 5 before any plant of the field was in the earth and before any herb of the field had grown. For the Lord God had not caused it to rain on the earth, and there was no man to till the ground; 6 but a mist went up from the earth and watered the whole face of the ground.

7 And the Jehovah formed man of the dust of the ground, and breathed into his nostrils the breath of life, and man became a living being.

Hold the phone! Chapter one, it clearly states that Elohim created herbs and plants and created man in his image, but now it says that there is not any of this?

It is clearly stated in chapter 1 that Elohim created herbs and plants and then created man in his image. But now, all of a sudden, there is no mention of any of this. This goes to show that the book of Genesis is not concerned with the realm of material science. It focuses solely on causation - the source of why things are. It is a spiritual, metaphysical book that delves into the subjective aspects of existence. According to this interpretation, once we align our subjective perceptions with truth, love, and life, everything else will naturally fall into place because the observer and the observed are one.

Elohim, also known as divine mind, creates through involution - ideating the universe and its perfect and whole ideas. These ideas are then brought into manifestation through Jehovah, I Am, Christ - the centralized presence of Elohim. However, it's important to note that we are still in the realm of the ideal at this point in time. As we will see in the next verse, God plants a garden in Eden where two trees grow: the tree of life and the tree of knowledge of good and evil.

This is not talking about corporeal trees with physical fruits that produce good and evil on this planet. Instead, it represents the garden of our soul, where these concepts exist on a spiritual level. The passage states that man was formed from dust - a substance that is fine and subtle, like air and earth, a multiplicity of forms unifying together. This speaks to us about etheric and atomic matter - reminding us that our soul acts as a gateway between the subtle spiritual and dense material dimensions.

According to 1 Corinthians 15:44, we have both natural bodies (physical) and spiritual bodies (soul). And 1 Corinthians 3:16 reminds us that our body is a temple for God's spirit to dwell within. When Jehovah breathes life into man, it is the inspiration of the spirit, energizing the soul and body and furthering the process of condensing spiritual ideals into physical form.

The presence of I Am, the true and palpable essence of Elohim, is not a mere name or word but a living and powerful force. Close your eyes and feel the stillness that surrounds you. Realize that you are not actively causing any of it - it simply exists all around you. A gentle, subtle hum of electric energy dances within and without, saturating every inch of your being. It is not produced by your thoughts or emotions; rather, it is the product of the infinite informational matrix that I Am. In reality, your consciousness does not belong to you at all. It exists within the boundless Ancient of Days, the ultimate Uberconsciousness - the I Am presence. No one can speak the words "I Am" for you; we are each unique manifestations of this sacred entity, and through us, I Am breathes divine inspiration into every moment. As Jesus said in John 15:5, "I am the vine; you are the branches. If you remain in me and I in you, you will bear much fruit; apart from me, you can do nothing." But let us take a step back. As we have discussed before, water represents the psychic realm, while rain symbolizes divine ideas falling from above and taking form in material substance. Spirit shapes the psychosphere, or "earth," which then molds and gives shape to this information. This process is often referred to as "the face of the earth" - the manifestation of spiritual substance in our souls. As spirit inspires our souls into action, things may seem unclear at first - like a mist slowly lifting to reveal God's concept for us.

8 The Lord God planted a garden eastward in Eden, and there He put the man whom He had formed. 9 And out of the ground, Jehovah made every tree grow that is pleasant to the sight and good for food. The tree of life was also in the midst of the garden and the tree of the knowledge of good and evil.

In the original Hebrew text, the "Garden of Eden" is referred to as "Gan Heden," which translates to an integrated sphere of organization and pleasure. This can be seen as a symbol for our own soul-sphere, connected to the source of life, Jehovah. Just as Jehovah created this organized realm of pleasure within us, he also planted a garden in the eastward region of Eden, representing our innermost being. The East represents the within, while the West represents the without. Our entire being is like an expansive garden, with the abode of God residing within us. It is the kingdom of heaven that Jesus spoke of when he said it is within us. A garden is a reflection of an ordered mind, and agriculture signifies our progression toward civilization through intentional and harmonious cultivation. Jehovah placed the elemental soul-sphere of humanity in this Garden, meaning our souls were once united with the source of all creation and pleasure - the kingdom of heaven on earth. Trees are a powerful symbol of the connection between heaven and earth, with their roots reaching deep into the intangible realm and branches extending outward into the tangible world. They stem from one unified trunk, branching out into multiplicity yet still remaining connected to its source. In the Garden, there were two trees - the Tree of Life and the Tree of knowledge of good and evil. These represent consuming truth and experiencing all that life has to offer. By consuming from the tree of life, we consume the ultimate truth that we are all projections of ONE divine entity, eternally connected with God. Those who consume from this tree will never taste death and will derive sustenance from all experiences on earth

10 Now a river went out of Eden to water the garden, and from there, it parted and became four river heads. 11 The name of the first is Pishon; it is the one which skirts the whole land of Havilah, where there is gold. 12 And the gold of that land is good. Bdellium and the onyx stone are there. 13 The name of the second river is Gihon; it is the one that goes around the whole land of Cush. 14 The name of the third river is Hiddekel; it is the one that goes toward the east of Assyria. The fourth river is the Euphrates.

Just as the tree is a singular entity that branches out into multiplicity, so do the four rivers described in Genesis, which originate from one source. The Bible utilizes numerology as a tool to deepen our understanding of its mysteries, and the number four symbolizes creation. On the fourth day, the material world is completed through the creation of the earth, and days five and six focus on populating this material ideal. This concept is reflected in the overlapping systems of our planet: earth (geosphere), air (atmosphere), water (hydrosphere), and living organisms (biosphere). The four elements - earth, air, fire, and water - also correspond to these systems. Additionally, there are four cardinal directions - north, south, east, and west. Likewise, there are four distinct seasons - winter, spring, summer, and autumn - signifying change and growth, death, new life, life, and dying. The natural world also reflects this numerical pattern with four kingdoms: mineral, plant, animal, and human. In Hebrew, the word for "river" used in this passage is "nahar," which shares the same root verb meaning "shine," "beam," "light," or "radiant flow." This further solidifies the idea that these rivers represent flows of energy and light. This further solidifies the idea that these rivers represent flows of energy and light. We see further confirmation of this concept in John 7:37-39 when Jesus speaks about those who believe in him receiving an innermost flow of living water from their hearts. This represents the Holy Spirit's revitalizing spiritual energy flowing within us. Just like how one river splits into four currents filled with creative power, the Holy Spirit brings vitality and abundance to all aspects of our lives.

Each river condenses into a sphere, pulsing with vibrant energy, as the completed menorah emerges. These "golden wheels" represent the four bodies - mechanical (physical), astral (desire body), mental (will), and causal (spiritual). Each body is like a shining piece in a grand puzzle, and that is our being. As we align with the life force of Elohim and dwell in Eden, we become projectors of divine wisdom. This wisdom, born from Christ consciousness, goes beyond earthly knowledge and manifests as intuition, judgment, and discernment. All four rivers burst forth from the one truth and source - the life and inspiration of God - flowing into even the furthest reaches of materiality. There is no separation between the spiritual and the material; they are intertwined and flow together as one. The first river, Pishon, the definition of which is full flowing, fully diffused, current energy, diffuses and spreads out the divine ideas of Jehovah, imparting them on all who encounter its current. The land it skirts, Havilah. Hivilah means to bring forth with effort, the struggle of elementary life, encompass, surround, and that there is gold in this land, which is good. This represents effort and struggle but also holds great treasures in the form of gold. This gold symbolizes the fruits of divine wisdom when used appropriately to navigate challenging situations. The second river, Gihon, is defined as bursting forth, gushing, and rapid stream, which rushes forth with unbridled energy - a rapid stream embracing the entire elemental body. As it flows around the land of Cush - representing materiality - it infuses love and light into every aspect of our being. Cush means burned, fire-like, blackened, darkness and represents materiality. Hiddekel, the third river, carries a universal generative fluid that brings continuous regeneration to our energetic system when aligned with Elohim's guidance. The definition of Hiddekel a universal generative fluid, rapid spiritual influx, and goes east toward Assyria. Assyria represents the sense world where reasoning often neglects cause for effect. However, when this river operates harmoniously with spirit - bringing continuous regeneration to our soul system - it becomes a powerful force for transformation. Finally, Euphrates completes this energetic complex by serving as a grounding and stabilizing force. Just as a four-sided structure is strong, balanced, equal, and stable, the fourth river holds together and aligns the other three currents, ensuring our soul system operates in unison. Its true role may be hidden, but its importance cannot be overstated. Therefore, not much other than the name is stated about Euphrates because the secret to its role is hidden in its fourth placement of the rivers and embodies the meaning of the number four we went over earlier.

15 Then the Lord God took the man and put him in the garden of Eden to tend and keep it. 16 And the Lord God commanded the man, saying, "Of every tree of the garden you may freely eat; 17 but

of the tree of the knowledge of good and evil you shall not eat, for in the day that you eat of it you shall surely die."

The garden of the soul must be tended and kept by man, a constant expansion of the original divine ideals set forth by Elohim in chapter one. We are the agriculturalists of the subtle realms, wielding tools such as thoughts, ideas, and imagination to shape our inner world. As we have briefly discussed, the tree of knowledge of good and evil holds the key to understanding the right relationship between spirit and matter, cause and effect. God is goodness itself, and all that he creates is inherently good. Goodness is light, and light brings order. Therefore, it follows that evil is disorder, chaos - and by partaking of the fruit from this forbidden tree, we are appropriating ideas of chaos into our souls. This is where we find the archaic term "demon." A demon is simply a manifestation of an individual's appropriation of the knowledge of evil. It is an idea that operates as an agent for chaos. Once we have ingested this knowledge of evil, it takes hold within us like a virus or parasitic infection - seeking to destroy all harmonious programs that allow us to function effectively in the spiritual, psychic, and material realms. This is why Jesus taught his disciples to cast out demons in his name - for Christ represents the light of the cosmos, bringing order to chaos and acting as an antidote against anti-order. As John 1:9 states, "That was the true Light which gives light to every man coming into the world." Thus, when we appropriate this psychic pathogen, Jehovah warns us that "we will surely die."

The forbidden fruit falls. Eve's teeth pierce the flesh as the juice drips down her chin. In this single bite, humanity has sealed its fate. The insidious knowledge creeps through their veins, a virus that will bring only chaos and death. But could this curse contain the key to salvation? Did the devil pull the wool over God's omniscient eyes and trick him, or was eating the tree the plan all along? The cosmic battle between order and chaos has begun in the Garden of Eden.

The tree of knowledge of good and evil represents our ability to understand and make choices between right and wrong. This was a necessary step in our journey towards spiritual growth - as we must be able to discern between what is beneficial for our souls and what is harmful. However, by choosing to partake in this knowledge without first seeking guidance from Elohim, we are appropriating ideas that are not aligned with divine order. And so, we'll see in just a few more passages that we will be expelled from the garden to work out our own salvation through time and space.

18 And the Lord God said, "It is not good that man should be alone; I will make him a helper comparable to him." 19 Out of the ground, the Lord God formed every beast of the field and every bird of the air, and brought them to Adam to see what he would call them. And whatever Adam called each living creature, that was its name. 20 So Adam gave names to all cattle, to the birds of the air, and to every beast of the field. ,However, for Adam, no helper comparable to him was found.

Again, in chapter one, Elohim already created beasts of the field and birds of the air. It is important to keep reminding ourselves that Genesis deals with stages of involution, which eventually unfold as evolution. As soul is subjective, whatever it observes it absorbs. Jehovah, I Am, works with Adam, wisdom-soul, to identify the various modes and animals, through which he will operate, referred to as his "helpers." Throughout all time, animals in cultures worldwide have been used as symbols to represent various aspects of our internal state. In the case of Genesis,, animals act as sensory circuits of our soul, expanding our psychosphere. Birds represent thoughts that act as mediators between our conscious and subconscious minds. Beasts represent strength, power, and vitality. Just as a Garden is the harmonious order of organic life forces, I Am illumination orders the psychosphere by allowing wisdom-soul, Adam, to identify and graph, the modes and functions through which the wisdom-soul will continue its development. Remember, Eden is the soul, and Adam is the wisdom of the soul as he arranges, identifies and organizes the Garden through breathing the continuous illumined inspiration of supraconsciousness, Jehovah. Adam, wisdom, the masculine principle, needs a helper who is equal in order to fully balance him out, just as the earth and moon balance each other.

21 And the Lord God caused a deep sleep to fall on Adam, and he slept, and He took one of his ribs, and closed up the flesh in its place. 22 Then the rib which the Lord God had taken from man He made into a woman, and He brought her to the man. 23 And Adam said: "This is now bone of my bones And flesh of my flesh; She shall be called Woman, Because she was taken out of Man." 24 Therefore, a man shall leave his father and mother and be joined to his wife, and they shall become one flesh. 25 And they were both naked, the man and his wife, and were not ashamed.

Each sphere of creation overlaps with the one below it, forming a beautiful and complex pattern. In mystic Judaism, Kabbalah refers to this process of the condensation of creation as the four worlds. In descending order, first is the world of Atziluth or World of Emanation. This is the archetype world of divine ideals. Next is Briah, or the World of Patterns. This is where ideals begin to draw patterns with each other, forming networks or a cosmic blueprint. Third is the Yetzirah, which is the World of Activity, where these ideas are now a matrix and begin to take individualized form. And lastly, the Fourth World, called Assiah, the World of Form, this is our day-to-day world, the realm of Malkuth, which means the Kingdom. The final and physical, or densest world, has its origin in Atziluth. As we descend through these layers, the once subtle energy fields begin to take on more distinct forms, creating a new vehicle for the Adamic cosmic male principle to function. This finely tuned essence served as a vessel for Elohim's divine conceptions in higher realms, but here in the denser spheres of creation, there is a necessity for Eve - a substance made from Adam's very energy - to be drawn out. She is known as the "mother of all living," for she represents the merging of masculine and feminine principles that are needed for creation to thrive.

Just as humanity is a microcosm of the entire universe, we can look at our own planet as an example. Here on Earth, we have two magnets - the north and south poles - which create a continuous magnetic flux. The energy lines that emerge from the north pole enter into the south pole, forming a protective field that shields us from harmful space radiation. This can help us understand how Adam's active energy must be balanced by drawing out its latent receptive counterpart.

Adam, representing wisdom and intellect, needs to be balanced by love. In order for soul unfoldment to reach its full potential, God's love must have a way to operate within us. And so, just as Adam was put into a deep sleep so that his mind could descend into unconsciousness and allow love to form within him, so too must the feminine aspect be crystallized into a denser manifestation.

We see evidence of this in Genesis chapter one when it says, "male and female created He them." The prototype of woman, the cosmic feminine, was already formed in the divine mind; now, as the cosmic man was crystalized into denser form, the feminine must follow suit, too.

And lo, the curious notion arises that a woman is crafted from a man's rib, a thought many scoff at and find absurd. But these words are not meant to be taken literally, for they evoke images in our minds that tap into deeper, primal truths beyond mere language. The Hebrew term used for "rib" is "tsela," which also means to bend or curve, implying a balance and equality between two opposing forces. As Saint Augustine proclaimed, if God intended for woman to rule over man, she would have been made from his head if she was meant to be his slave, she would have come from his feet. But instead, she was formed from his side, a symbol of her equal partnership with man. And just as the nucleus of an atom contains positively charged protons and neutral neutrons, balanced by negatively charged electrons swirling around them, so too do the principles of masculine and feminine, wisdom and love, exist on both the cosmic and atomic levels. While Adam sleeps, representing the unconscious intellect, Jehovah (I Am) brings forth Eve (love), uniting the two in perfect harmony. And it is through this union that they are able to express the higher consciousness of Jehovah in greater ways. Notice that while Jehovah puts Adam to sleep (rendering his intellect unconscious), it never says that He wakes him up. This signifies that Adam's limited understanding of Jehovah led him to fall into unconsciousness until Eve (love) was formed to balance him out. Together, they represent the original state of divine love and wisdom working together in perfect harmony. And it is from this state of unity that all true love comes forth from Jehovah and impresses upon the elemental world. As it was in the beginning before the fall of man, when Adam and Eve were naked and unashamed - symbolizing their pure psychological state before any sense of a personal self had developed.

And so it was that Adam and Eve lived in perfect union with Jehovah, free from any sense of a personal self. Without this false, limited identity, they were plugged directly into the mind of God and could receive limitless revelation and illumination. They were unashamed, for their only identity was the I Am, the capital I of God.

In this state, there was no need for clothing or material possessions, for they lacked nothing. They were provided for by the divine mind and lived in perfect harmony with nature. Their consciousness was pure and innocent, devoid of any egoic desires or fears.

The Fall Of Humanity - Genesis Chapter 3

3Now, the serpent was more subtle than any other wild creature that Jehovah had made. He said to the woman, "Did God say, 'You shall not eat of any tree of the garden?" And the woman said to the serpent, "We may eat of the fruit of the trees of the garden; but God said, 'You shall not eat of the fruit of the tree which is the midst of the garden, neither shall you touch it, lest you die." But the serpent said to the woman, "You will not die. For God knows that when you eat of it, your eyes will be opened, and you will be like God, knowing good and evil." So when the woman saw that the tree was good for food and that it was a delight to the eyes, and that the tree was to be desired to make one wise, she took of its fruit and ate; and she also gave some to her husband, and he ate. Then the eyes of both were opened, and they knew that they were naked, and they sewed fig leaves together and made themselves aprons.

In this third chapter of Genesis, the serpent represents the temptations of earthly pleasures that lure us away from our spiritual nature. This serpent is described as being more subtle than any other wild creature that Jehovah had made, indicating its clever and cunning nature.

The serpent first questions the woman about God's command not to eat from the Tree of Knowledge of good and evil. The woman responds by stating that they may eat from any tree in the garden except for this one, and they must not even touch it, or they will die. The serpent then tells her that she will not die, but rather, her eyes will be opened, and she will become like God, knowing good and evil.

The woman is enticed by the thought of gaining wisdom and becoming like God, so she eats the fruit from the forbidden tree and gives some to her husband as well. As a result, their eyes are opened, and they become aware of their nakedness. In an attempt to cover themselves and hide their shame, they sew fig leaves together to make aprons.

This story symbolizes the fall of humanity from a state of pure consciousness into a limited state of individualized egoic awareness. By succumbing to the temptation of earthly desires, Adam and Eve separated themselves from Jehovah and their true divine identity.

Their eyes were opened not in a positive sense but rather in a negative one – they became aware of their own personal selves rather than being plugged into the mind of God. They now saw themselves as separate beings with individual desires and needs instead of being united with Jehovah in pure love.

With this knowledge also came shame – they felt exposed in their vulnerability without clothes or possessions to define them. So, they covered themselves up with fig leaves, symbolizing how we use material possessions to mask our insecurities and false identities.

It is like a corrupted computer program infecting our divine code, masking our true beauty and purpose. Our soul becomes coated in a layer of falsehoods and illusions, disconnecting us from the true source of meaning and life - God. This is the root of the fall of man, as Eve succumbed to the seductions of the physical world and allowed them to taint her love soul.

In the beginning, Adam possessed great intelligence and a pure love for his Creator. But when he was tempted by the fruit of knowledge, he consumed it, and this led to the manifestation of evil, the distortion of reality. As spiritual teacher Gurdjieff wisely said, knowledge alone is not enough for true understanding. True understanding comes from aligning our knowledge with our being. It is important to remember that matter itself is not inherently evil; it is simply a denser form of spiritual energy created by Elohim. It only becomes 'evil' when we forget its true nature and mistake it for ultimate reality. This delusion leads to suffering and death as we cut ourselves off from the eternal life that comes from Elohim. A perfect example of this fallen state of consciousness can be seen in addiction, where the desire for external stimuli can never be truly satisfied because true satisfaction can only come from the source - spirit. This concept is reflected in quantum mechanics, where matrix theory suggests that spacetime is pixelated and our three-dimensional reality is actually made up of indivisible units, much like a two-dimensional TV screen. Meaning and feeling aren't derived from the individual pixels making up the picture; and they are derived from the intention that is projected through the pixels.

Instead of a unified omniconsciousness, we now fall into a dualistic, compartmentalized consciousness, not just knowing good and life, but knowing and therefore experiencing evil, which leads to death. Through this conscious appropriation of no-thing evil, into ourselves, a separation from uniconsciousness creeps into our psyche. This split is the separation of the conscious and subconscious, which were once unified by the firmament, "the eyes of both of them were opened, and they knew they were naked." No longer one soul being harmonized by the firmament, Heaven, now each sees themselves naked, aware of their separate psychological functions, as we discussed clothes represent. "They sewed fig leaves together and made aprons," this tells us that once when their generative functions were in symphony together, represented by the genitals and apron covering, there is now dissonance, and the natural state that follows this is the clashing of two non-unified forces. The fig leaves are also the first account of technology, clothes being one of the oldest technologies. The attempt to cover themselves with fig leaves is the attempt to create a protective layer around themselves in order to 'hide themselves' from what they perceive now as a separate entity, Jehovah.

8 And they heard the sound of the Lord God walking in the garden in the cool of the day, and Adam and his wife hid themselves from the presence of the Lord God among the trees of the garden.

9 Then the Lord God called to Adam and said to him, "Where are you?" 10 So he said, "I heard Your voice in the garden, and I was afraid because I was naked; and I hid myself." 11 And He said, "Who told you that you were naked? Have you eaten from the tree of which I commanded you that you should not eat?" 12 Then the man said, "The woman whom You gave to be with me, she gave me of the tree, and I ate." 13 And the Lord God said to the woman, "What is this you have done?" The woman said, "The serpent deceived me, and I ate." 14 So the Lord God said to the serpent: "Because you have done this, You are cursed more than all cattle, And more than every beast of the field; On your belly you shall go, And you shall eat dust All the days of your life. 15 And I will put enmity Between you and the woman, and between your seed and her Seed; He shall bruise your head, and you shall bruise His heel."

16 To the woman He said: "I will greatly multiply your sorrow and your conception; In pain you shall bring forth children; Your desire shall be for your husband, And he shall rule over you."17 Then to Adam He said, "Because you have heeded the voice of your wife, and have eaten from the tree of which I commanded you, saying, 'You shall not eat of it': "Cursed is the ground for your sake;

In toil you shall eat of it All the days of your life. 18 Both thorns and thistles it shall bring forth for you, and you shall eat the herb of the field. 19 In the sweat of your face you shall eat bread Till you return to the ground, For out of it you were taken; For dust you are, And to dust you shall return." 20 And Adam called his wife's name Eve, because she was the mother of all living. 21 Also for Adam and his wife the Lord God made tunics of skin and clothed them.

22 Then the Lord God said, "Behold, the man has become like one of Us, to know good and evil. And now, lest he put out his hand and take also of the tree of life, and eat, and live forever"— 23 therefore the Lord God sent him out of the garden of Eden to till the ground from which he was taken. 24 So He drove out the man; and He placed cherubim at the east of the garden of Eden, and a flaming sword which turned every way, to guard the way to the tree of life.

The tone of Jehovah's voice was intense and harsh as he dished out the new laws. The author of Genesis used this tone purposefully, wanting to make it clear that an antagonistic perception of God had been solidified in our consciousness. As we descended through the spheres of creation - from causal, to subtle, to mental, and finally to bodily - a constriction of consciousness also took place. Life is I Am, Jehovah - the ever-living One - and even in our constricted state, his presence remains with us, giving life to all things. However, instead of knowing only good, we now also know evil because I Am is life itself. By knowing evil, we give it power and this sets us on a path of regression. Instead of ascending from causal to body as intended, we must now ascend through the sequence of body, mental, subtle, and finally back to causal. "No one has ever gone into heaven except the one who came from heaven - the Son of Man," John 3:13. It tells us that Jehovah walked in the cool of the day, but when we are consumed by passion, we slip into unconscious mechanical behavior. Our rational brain takes a backseat and our primal instincts, called the reptilian brain, take over - instincts for feeding, fighting, fleeing, and reproduction - represented by the serpent who deceived us. After we have satisfied our lust and returned to a state of levelheadedness, there is an immediate switch that marks the genesis of the personal self. Adam and Eve suddenly believe they can hide from the omniscience and omnipresence of Jehovah, a belief that will ultimately lead to suffering, sin, sickness, and death. In order for them to believe they can hide themselves from God's knowledge and presence, they must first be under the delusion that they are separate entities with their own personal space - something God cannot access or understand. When Jehovah asks, "who told you that you were naked?" he is getting at the root of what the serpent, Satan, the devil, represents throughout the Bible - adversary and accuser. The serpent accuses Adam and Eve of being naked - of being different from God. From this point on, God curses the serpent to crawl on its belly and eat the dust of the earth; a symbolic connection between our desire for material satisfaction and our soul, for Genesis also tell us that we are formed of the dust of the earth (Genesis 2:7) so Satan is our sense consciousness that can never find satisfaction and peace. We are constantly craving material things because we have been fused with the material dimension, but ultimate peace can only be found by uniting with omni-consciousness - with Jehovah. This is the enmity between the serpent and the woman: Eve's desire body longs for unification with first cause - love/Jehovah - but while trapped in the three-dimensional world of materiality, she will never find it as the serpent's duty is to keep us in continuous dissatisfaction because his appetite for the dust, we are made of is insatiable.

In the tranquil garden of the soul, God presided over the creation of the laws that would shape the three-dimensional world of spacetime - the most solid and tangible sphere of existence. As the serpent, Eve, and Adam coexisted as distinct but intertwined functions of one androgynous being, they were given a divine decree: "Your desire will be for your husband." However, this declaration has been misconstrued by literalists for centuries, leading to unjust persecution of women. In truth, it represents the inevitable disconnect between intellect (Adam) and desire (Eve) in mankind's consciousness - a dissonance between head and heart, conscious and subconscious. Though rationality, logic, and reason are powerful assets, they can also cause chaos, pain, and suffering when elevated above love, emotion, and feeling - represented by Eve. The pains of childbirth symbolize this struggle between aligning with the flow of life from the source vs. striving against it. For consciousness is an embodiment of love - not just in the sense of romantic gestures or lavish displays, but at its core essence as a reconciling force. It is the substance that harmonizes and brings order to all other elements, as exemplified by Christ's proclamation that "God is love." Now that Adam and Eve have become disconnected from their source of unity (love), all things come through strife and struggle. This same antagonistic relationship between serpent and woman reappears in the climactic finale of Revelation chapter 12: a woman cloaked in sunlight stands upon a moon with twelve stars encircling her head as she labors to give birth to her child. At her feet lurks a great red dragon waiting to devour her newborn at any moment. This scene represents the culmination of humanity's journey towards spiritual awakening - where the seed of Eve (the human race) has flourished across all lands while the once-humble serpent from Genesis has transformed into a colossal devouring dragon, embodying the collective egoic force that stands in opposition to I AM. The book of Revelation is a powerful display of potent symbolism that unlocks deep and primal spiritual forces within us - not to be taken literally. The woman in labor symbolizes the cosmic mother, Eve - mother of all living beings who have mastered the elemental forces and is now ready to give birth to a new state of Christ consciousness: complete unity with Jehovah once more. The dragon, or serpent, represents the accuser, the adversary - the false self that perceives itself as the ultimate cause and is adversarial towards God. In summary, we see the ongoing struggle of the soul to rise above perceived separation and reunite with God after the fall. As Jehovah imparts his laws for functioning in this next sphere of creation (spacetime), he declares that "in toil, you shall eat," implying a disconnection from our intrinsic connection with earth experienced in higher realms and descent into denser forms that create an illusion of separation. This leads to antagonistic actions towards all perceived separate entities as the rational mind becomes detached from desire and works mechanically to dissect, manipulate, and control through force. And thus, the earth is seen as hostile and uncooperative - producing thorns and thistles. Ultimately, Jehovah warns Adam that partaking of the tree of Life would result in eternal existence in this fragmented state, apart from true unity with God, which would lead to eternal damnation and hell, but God's will is that all be saved, and none shall perish (2 Peter 3:9).

Jehovah, I Am, then states, "Behold, the man has become like one of Us, to know good and evil. And now, lest he put out his hand and take also of the tree of life, and eat, and live forever."

Adam and Eve, now in a state of adverse and detached consciousness, are infected with the belief that evil is a force unto itself - the opposite of God and life itself. They are warned not to eat from the tree of life, for if they do, they will be trapped forever in an eternal downward spiral of suffering. To prevent this fate, Jehovah casts them out of the garden and away from his presence, giving them the freedom to work through their false belief in duality within themselves.

After gaining a state of consciousness that clouds their divine nature, they are now tasked with tilling the ground from which they originated in order to uncover and reclaim their true divine essence. The Garden of Eden represents a perfect balance and harmony between spiritual ideas and their symbiotic connection with the source. However, Adam and Eve have lost sight of this and must now struggle and strive to make progress on their path instead of experiencing effortless flow. As they leave, Jehovah provides them with tunics made of animal skin, symbolizing their first physical bodies. No longer one being, Adam and his wife are now divided into two separate entities, only vaguely remembering their previous unified state. Clothed in these new bodies and equipped with a deeper understanding of the laws governing three-dimensional reality, they venture out into the world of illusion known as spacetime.

Leaving the garden also means leaving the presence of God and living under the false belief that they are disconnected from Him, trapped in their own individual reality. This leads to a linear progression of thoughts, feelings, and desires as they strive for understanding, with the ultimate goal of returning to Eden and consuming the tree of life. Jesus has achieved this, and it is our own life purpose to follow in his footsteps, for he is the path. The entire Bible guides us through this journey of exploring our own consciousness until we merge back into unity with God by embracing spiritual truths and developing a personal relationship with Christ - our source of being. Paul explains who, being in very nature God, did not consider equality with God something to be used to his own advantage; rather, he made himself nothing by taking the very nature of a servant, being made in human likeness. (Philippians 2:6-7). This process culminates in Revelation where, after dying to ourselves (making ourselves nothing by taking on the heart of a servant) and being reborn in Christ, a New Heaven and Earth are created with the tree of life at its core - sustaining those who partake for eternity.

Lastly, Jehovah places Cherubim at the east gate of the garden with a flaming sword to guard the way back to the Tree of Life. Cherubim symbolize protection and sacred life. They are first mentioned here to guard the gate into Eden with a flaming sword. Also, in Ezekiel they are the drivers of the Son of Man's chariot, where there are four of them, and there are two of them placed on top of the arch of the covenant. They are described in Ezekiel as having four faces - that of a man, lion, ox, and eagle. These represent different aspects of creation and humanity, offering insight into the path back to Eden. First to note is their four fold nature. This links them to our physical universe and the dynamic forces of the earth as we've discussed what the number four represents. It also links them to the four rivers flowing out of Eden, the four and the four Gospels.

To understand the riddle of the Cherubim is to discover the path back to Eden. Their fourfold nature represents the different spheres created by Elohim through Jehovah during the formation of the cosmic human - the causal, subtle, mental, and physical.

The face of the man represents the mental realm. As prototype man, Adam represented wisdom and intellect, the realm where the universe is mapped out, brought into a matrix of clarity, and named the animals. The lion represents the subtle or astral realm, as the lion is used to symbolize untamed strength, courage, independence, and majesty. It can also symbolize latent passions and desire and correlates to the desire-body, or subtle realm. The ox represents the physical, corporeal realm, as the ox must be domesticated to help bring in a harvest. It represents the first stage and first realm we must transcend for as the ox must be disciplined to reap a harvest so too must our physical body. The eagle represents the ideal realm, subject to no one, prey to no one. The eagle saws high above all, in the firmament, Heaven and therefore represents the ideal realm of spiritual ideas. The Cherubim is placed at the east side of Eden, meaning within, just as the sun rises in the east and dissolves the darkness of night our spiritual insight brings light to our lives from within. This Cherubim is given a flaming sword that turns everyway, which represents spiritual truth that can be deadly when approached with an earthly, fallen state of consciousness. We must re-spiritualize our being through meditation on spiritual thoughts, mediation and prayer by doing so, we shed off the skins of the old realms and steadily evolve, ascend back up through the realms of creation until we awaken to the truth that "I and the father are ONE," John 10:30. Luckily Jesus already did this, and as Adam was the cosmic man and therefore all of humanity fell when Adam fell, Jesus is the representative of the human race, and all can ascend through him. The Apostle Paul puts it as, "For Christ's love compels us, because we are convinced that one died for all, and therefore all died." Notice it is Christ's love that compels us. Love is the golden thread that enables us to traverse the realms; it is the great river of life that we travel on, love, the energy highway we ride through the lower realms until we merge back into supraconsiousness. Eden is complete unity with the presence of God, and just as we descended away from God's presence through the various realms, we must ascend back through those realms by letting "thine eye be single," Mathew 6:22, no-longer perceiving life through a dualistic state of mind. Once we have done this, we will realize that the Cherubim is a holographic representation of the journey of the path our souls have taken and, therefore, will no-longer be an obstruction to the presence of God and the tree of life.

4 Now Adam knew Eve, his wife, and she conceived and bore Cain, and said, "I have acquired a man from the Lord." 2 Then she bore again, this time his brother Abel. Now Abel was a keeper of sheep, but Cain was a tiller of the ground. 3 And in the process of time, it came to pass that Cain brought an offering of the fruit of the ground to the Lord. 4 Abel also brought of the firstborn of his flock and of their fat. And the Lord respected Abel and his offering,

5 but He did not respect Cain and his offering. And Cain was very angry, and his countenance fell. 6 So the Lord said to Cain, "Why are you angry? And why has your countenance fallen? 7 If you do well, will you not be accepted? And if you do not do well, sin lies at the door. And its desire is for you, but you should rule over it."8 Now Cain talked with Abel, his brother, and it came to pass, when they were in the field, that Cain rose up against Abel, his brother and killed him.9 Then the Lord said to Cain, "Where is Abel, your brother?"

He said, "I do not know. Am I my brother's keeper?" 10 And He said, "What have you done? The voice of your brother's blood cries out to Me from the ground. 11 So now you are cursed from the earth, which has opened its mouth to receive your brother's blood from your hand. 12 When you till the ground, it shall no longer yield its strength to you. A fugitive and a vagabond you shall be on the earth." 13 And Cain said to the Lord, "My punishment is greater than I can bear! 14 Surely You have driven me out this day from the face of the ground; I shall be hidden from Your face; I shall be a fugitive and a vagabond on the earth, and it will happen that anyone who finds me will kill me." 15 And the Lord said to him, "Therefore, whoever kills Cain, vengeance shall be taken on him sevenfold." And the Lord set a mark on Cain, lest anyone finding him should kill him.

Cain points out the contradiction in this statement, "Anyone who finds me will kill me." Wait a minute, I thought there were only four people in this story, and one of them was just killed. Once again, we see that the book of Genesis is not a literal history textbook about the physical creation of the earth. Instead, it is a mysterious and meaningful book about humanity and our relationship with God and all of creation. The name Cain means possession, acquisition, sharpness, cutting, or like a lance. He is the first child born to Adam and Eve after they came together again. From the very beginning, we see that Cain is born into a mindset of separation - he desires what he thinks he may lose. On the other hand, their second child, Abel, means breath or something transitory. This child represents the divided consciousness of Adam and Eve: one side is possessive and deluded by separation, and the other side represents the spiritual realm through its connection to the soul. We can remember that when Jehovah breathed into Adam's nostrils, he became a living soul - showing us that Abel represents the subtle aspect of humanity that connects us to both the soul and the spirit. In contrast, Cain represents the fallen and isolated side of our dualistic nature. This reversal goes against Elohim's creative process, where spiritual ideals come first; instead, we experience the natural and earthly ideas that lead to death first.

It is worth noting that throughout the first three chapters of Genesis, time is not mentioned, but as soon as Adam and Eve are cast out of the Garden of Eden and into the realm of spacetime, it is brought up in one of the first sentences, "and in the process of time" (Genesis 4:3). This signifies the start of humanity's evolutionary journey. It mentions that Abel was a keeper of sheep and Cain was a tiller of the ground. In this allegory, animals represent different emotional qualities within ourselves. As a shepherd who cares for and develops a loving relationship with his sheep, Abel represents our ability to work with volition and emotions. On the other hand, Cain deals with mechanical vegetable life, where there is no free will or emotional connection. This can be seen as a reflection of Adam and Eve; Adam represents logical reasoning while Eve embodies emotion and feeling. When God created "man" in their image, it says, "male and female created he them." So even though in chapter two, Eve seems to come after Adam, in the ideal prototype realm of chapter one they were created simultaneously. However, in the realm of spacetime, this order is inverted, and Cain, representing cold rationality, is born before Abel, who embodies warmth and unity. The functions of the mind dissect and analyze while emotions bring together and build through relationships. This is why God favored Abel's sacrifice over Cain's - because genuine emotion and love are essential for connecting with God. When we give without seeking personal gain, we take on the nature of God who infinitely gives to all. Abel's offering of his first-born sheep is considered pleasing because it is an emotional sacrifice; he offers something that he has developed a loving relationship with as opposed to Cain who simply crops the harvest mechanically.

Our connection with God cannot be attained through analytical thinking alone. It is through our volition, feelings, and emotions that we truly commune with , Him, a realm of the subconscious mind. The universe is a complex web of relationships and interdependence. A forest serves as an example, where hub trees provide more sugar than they need through photosynthesis, which feeds fungi through their root system. In turn, the fungi form a network with threads called mycelium, allowing for efficient nutrient absorption by all the trees in the forest. This symbiotic relationship illustrates how interconnected and reliant the entire system is. The same can be said for our bodies and even the solar system. When we consider quantum entanglement alongside the Big Bang theory, it becomes clear that everything is intrinsically linked within an interconnected hierarchy. When we live from this understanding, we can be in constant communion with God and see ourselves as part of something greater. Our perspective shifts from possessiveness to cooperation, leading to a fuller experience of life and ultimately bringing us closer to God. Knowing that we are one with Jehovah and intrinsically connected to Him allows us to realize that we are not living life, but life is living us.

16 Then Cain went out from the presence of the Lord and dwelt in the land of Nod on the east of Eden. 17 And Cain knew his

wife, and she conceived and bore Enoch. And he built a city, and called the name of the city after the name of his son—Enoch

Cain travels to the land of Nod. Nod, in Hebrew, means to wonder with uncertainty. Our emotional body is the driving force behind all action in life. Before we act on anything, a certain measure of passion and feeling must spark within us to ignite action. Since Cain, the rational mind, killed the ability for passion, he wanders aimlessly through life with no certain destination as he has no emotional attachment and feels no relation to any specific thing. The world becomes void of meaning. It is said that he knew his wife and they had a son named Enoch. There is hope for Cain as he finds a wife; once again, the feminine represents the emotional body. However, he finds this wife in the earth and is therefore of the earth, not of divine causation; it is a secondary effect. True repentance is never spoken with the mouth or thought out in the head; it is deeply felt in the heart, the subconscious system. Only this way do we experience a true psychological shift, which is what the word metanoia means: to change your mind and repent. This is how Cain found a wife; after this repentance, the emotional body was kindled once more but it was not the originating soul body of first cause; it did not come from Adam and Eve; it was the second cause produced from the earth. This first son is not the famous Enoch that most people know but this Enoch's name means founder, centralizer, contrition, repentance. And here we see once more that Cain was indeed forgiven of his sin toward his brother Abel; for his offspring, that which came out of him, represents a mind state of repentance which is the prerequisite for forgiveness. Though Cain was forgiven by Jehovah and given a mark which renders Karmic law null, he is still locked into the delusion of separation from God.

Now, this is where it gets interesting: it says that Cain built a city. What is a city? A city is a hyper-realization of our individual private selves on a collective scale. It is a system with boundaries and borders, isolated, closed off from agriculture, the natural world, and work. It is a condensed system of housing, business, government organizations, etc. that perpetuates commerce and strains natural resources. But none of it has any grounding in reality.

As the philosopher Baudrillard would put it, it is the hyper-real, a simulation of a reality of which the origins have been forgotten. If I offered a bear one hundred dollars to not eat me, he would just bite off my hand that holds the bill. Money and the entire system are illusionary and only have meaning because of the value we give them. The personal self is exactly the same.

The Tim Carpenter part of me is just a matrix of memories, desires, dislikes, stories I repeatedly tell myself, and so on. It is a societal construct that perceives itself as separate and wholly other than everyone else – a private and personal self. It forever veils our vision with thoughts and feelings of past programs and future uncertainties and, therefore never allows us to truly experience the only true reality: now.

This private and personal self is illusionary; the real self that I am is I AM – that living substance within which all information that builds up the walls of Tim Carpenter's personal self exists within.

This is what Apostle Paul meant when he said in 1 Corinthians 15:31: "I affirm by boasting in you which I have in Christ Jesus our Lord – I die daily." It is this world identity – the virtual self – that we must die to daily and remember that the life we are living is the crystallization of ONE life, which is Jehovah.

From this fallen state of mind – the fragmented self – it is natural for Cain to build the first city because once again a city is just an amplification of this separate self-consciousness that shuts itself off from natural law – a severing from organic symbiotic consciousness to that of detachment and isolation.

Just go to any city's center – its heart –, and you will see a mass concentration of addiction, disease, violence, perversion, suffering pain – all manifestations of a virtual self that lives under the delusion that it is isolated, cut off from source withers dies just as a flower when cut from stem.

With this knowledge of what the separate self is and how cities are extension magnifications of this separate self, we can tackle the rest of the book.

OLD TESTAMENT GOD VS NEW TESTAMENT GOD

In the ongoing debate between believers and non-believers, one argument frequently arises: why does a supposedly loving God display such violence, jealousy, and malice in the Old Testament? Even among believers, there is confusion as to why the God of the New Testament seems so different from the God of the Old. However, these questions stem from a fundamental misunderstanding of the nature of God and his embodiment through Jesus.

As Jesus himself proclaims, the most important law is found in Deuteronomy 6:4 - "Hear, O Israel: The Lord our God, the Lord is one." This statement emphasizes the unity and interconnectedness of all things under one life force rather than a fragmented reality where individual forms are seen as separate entities. But it was not until Moses encountered the burning bush and learned that God's true nature is "I AM WHO I AM," Yahweh, that humanity began to understand this concept.

Moses, who was raised in Pharaoh's household and exposed to Egypt's powerful spiritual system, saw how this knowledge had been distorted over time. The symbols and idols that once represented deeper truths were now worshipped themselves, with mortals like pharaohs being elevated to god-like status. This corruption of spiritual understanding led to further division and suffering.

This gradual evolution of human consciousness can be traced throughout the Bible, from Adam and Eve's preconscious state in Eden to Cain's dualistic mindset to Moses' superpersonal revelation of I Am to Jesus' complete embodiment of Christ's consciousness. Understanding this helps us reconcile the seemingly contradictory portrayals of God in the Old and New Testaments.

To get a firmer grasp of this concept, we need to take a look at the famous story of Moses and the burning bush. It is the moment when Moses awakens to the truth that the name of God, the nature of God, is I AM WHO I AM, Yahweh. Once again, the Bible is the story of the evolution of the human soul, or stages of humanities conscious evolution, from Adam and Eve's preconscious symbiotic state in Eden, to Cain's personal, dualistic, fragmented state to Moses' superpersonal revelation of I Am, to Jesus embodiment and complete personification of I Am, Christ consciousness. Understanding this will help us understand the seeming contradictions between the Old and New Testament God.

We may all know that Moses was raised by Pharaoh's daughter and brought up in the Pharaoh's household as an Egyptian, so he was well versed in the religious beliefs and laws of Egypt. At that time, Egypt was the most powerful religious civilization and had developed a powerful and intricate spiritual system. However, over time, the secrets of the Egyptian mysteries and those who were supposed to be keepers of this knowledge lost sight of its true essence and symbols, statues, idols and images that once were understood to simply be symbolic representations of greater and deeper truths became the object of worship themselves. And the greater spiritual meanings behind these symbols were lost. The Pharaohs, though just mortal men and women, were proclaimed to be a deity and all glory, honor and worship should be attributed to them.

We see in the case of Jesus, the King of Kings, that with every word, every action, and miracle he did, he attributed to Father God. Always in every case giving glory and honor to God and never to his personal, Jesus of Nazareth self. "I can of Myself do nothing. As I hear, I judge; and My judgment is righteous, because I do not seek My own will but the will of the Father who sent Me," John 5:30. "You heard me say, 'I am going away, and I am coming back to you.' If you loved me, you would be glad that I am going to the Father, for the Father is greater than I," John 14:28. This is a stark contrast to all other kings, rulers, Pharaohs and the like throughout history. By attributing all things he did to the Father, God, Jesus is letting us know that this power that he personified is accessible to all, unlike all the other rulers who hoarded the knowledge to themselves so that their mortal selves would be exalted and worshiped. "Most assuredly, I say to you, he who believes in Me, the works that I do he will do also; and greater works than these he will do, because I go to My Father," John 14:12.

Some groundwork needed to be laid down in preparation for the leap in conscious evolution that Jesus displayed, and so Moses revelation was a starting point, a key that would begin to set people free spiritually, which in turn would manifest naturally, namely the liberation of the Israelites from slavery in Egypt. A departure from the dualistic restraints and dominance that the worship of the material, corporeal bound them to (Egypt) into an awakening of non-dualistic unification in the subtler realms of consciousness (I AM). So, let us study the account of Moses' great revelation, which will eventually give us a good understanding of why the Old Testament God seems so different from the New. In Exodus 3, we read the account of Moses' great moment of enlightenment, where he encounters the burning bush.

"Now Moses was tending the flock of Jethro, his father-in-law, and the priest of Midian. And he led the flock to the back of the desert and came to Horeb, the mountain of God. And the Angel of the Lord appeared to him in a flame of fire from the midst of a bush. So, he looked, and behold, the bush was burning with fire, but the bush was not consumed. Then Moses said, "I will now turn aside and see this great sight, why the bush does not burn."

When the Lord saw that he turned aside to look, God called to him from the midst of the bush and said, "Moses, Moses!" And he said, "Here I am." Then He said, "Do not draw near this place. Take your sandals off your feet, for the place where you stand is holy ground." 6 Moreover, He said, "I am the God of your father—the God of Abraham, the God of Isaac, and the God of Jacob." And Moses hid his face, for he was afraid to look upon God. And the Lord said: "I have surely seen the oppression of My people who are in Egypt and have heard their cry because of their taskmasters, for I know their sorrows. 8 So I have come down to deliver them out of the hand of the Egyptians, and to bring them up from that land to a good and large land, to a land flowing with milk and honey, to the place of the Canaanites and the Hittites and the Amorites and the Perizzites and the Hivites and the Jebusites. 9 Now therefore, behold, the cry of the children of Israel has come to Me, and I have also seen the oppression with which the Egyptians oppress them. 10 Come now, therefore, and I will send you to Pharaoh that you may bring My people, the children of Israel, out of Egypt." But Moses said to God, "Who am I that I should go to Pharaoh and that I should bring the children of Israel out of Egypt?" So, He said, "I will certainly be with you. And this shall be a sign to you that I have sent you: When you have brought the people out of Egypt, you shall serve God on this mountain." Then Moses said to God, "Indeed when I come to the children of Israel and say to them, 'The God of your fathers has sent me to you,' and they say to me, 'What is His name?' what shall I say to them?" And God said to Moses, "I AM WHO I AM." And He said, "Thus you shall say to the children of Israel, 'I AM has sent me to you." 15 Moreover, God said to Moses, "Thus you shall say to the children of Israel: 'The Lord God of your fathers, the God of Abraham, the God of Isaac, and the God of Jacob, has sent me to you. This is My name forever, and this is My memorial to all generations.'

The name Moses means to draw out of water. Water, along with representing the psyche and mind, also represents chaos or unknown potentiality. We each have that spark of life within us that seeks to know and understand God more. Moses mission individually and universally was to draw out and establish a firmament, a firm foundation of truth on which the new nation of the people of I AM, (Israelites) could stand. He is the evolutionary upward pull within each one of us that unravels the knowledge of God we each have coiled up inside.

He is tending Jethro's flock. Jethro was a priest, and Moses was a spiritual teacher and mentor. Sheep in the bible represent thoughts, so he is meditating on the holy thoughts taught to him by his Priest, Jethro. He goes up the mountain of Herob. Herob means silence and a mountain represents the highest place in consciousness, the emergence of personal to transpersonal awareness. The base of a mountain is wide and undefined, but as we ascend the mountain, all things gradually become clearer until, at the very top, we come to a unified point, and all things become visible to us. We can read this then as Moses being in an ascended, transpersonal state of consciousness, meditating on his oneness with God when a burning bush is presented to him.

The bush is burning but is not consumed. A bush represents wood. The Greeks, through Aristotle, had no word for corporeal matter, so they adopted the word hyle, which means wood, as they believed that all physical things are made of the same basic substance. So, the Greek word for wood is synonymous with matter. We can read this then as matter was consumed by spiritual energy and here lies the epiphany. Fire is repeatedly used to represent the spirit of God throughout the bible because fire transmutes the nature of material substance from dense to subtle. The flames of fire are matter, but the light and heat that come from a fire are energy. The very nature of fire is to transmute dense matter into a finer, more energetic substance. However, it says that this fire did not consume the bush. This is because the energy of God, the originating substance, is life itself, and instead of destroying, it renews, animates and purifies. This is telling us that there is a emergence of spirit and matter into one. Moses is seeing past the material veil and now sees with clarity the true nature of the universe, which is that all things are soaking in the living spiritual substance of God, which animates all.

An Angel of Jehovah speaks to Moses from this state of supraconsciousness and tells him to remove his sandals. Firstly, Moses questions who he is to be tasked with such a mission. He is thinking from his limited, fragmented self. Then Moses said to God, "Indeed, when I come to the children of Israel and say to them, 'The God of your fathers has sent me to you,' and they say to me, 'What is His name?' what shall I say to them?" And God said to Moses, "I AM WHO I AM." And He said, "Thus you shall say to the children of Israel, 'I AM has sent me to you. "God reminds him that it is not Moses who is going to do this, but that Moses is operating from the omniconscious, I AM presence. This name was given to Moses: I Am Who I Am. In Hebrew, it is Yahweh. It is not the name of a personal being, as that would imply limitation, but it stands as a statement of infinite self-aware presence within which all potentiality is contained. It is a statement of undifferentiated awareness, pure intelligence, and self-existent formless life, and when Yahweh communicates with us, the filter of our mind crystalizes the intention of God's ideal into a definite concept. This concept is wholistic and pure, direct from God and therefore perceived as an angel, as angels are messengers.

Secondly, the foot is the most external part of us in respect to that part of us that contacts the earth, and so a sandal or shoe esoterically symbolizes a covering or protection between us and the world (reality). It can be our pre-conceived notions, prejudices, beliefs developed from past experiences, ect. Overall, it can represent our various personas we pick and choose to embody depending on what encounter in the earth we have. This divine concept of Jehovah (angel) Moses is awakening to, tells Moses to remove this layer of self-protection because while still wearing them, he is living from a separate self-identity that prevents him from fully unifying with God and so Moses takes off his sandals and steps into non-dualistic consciousness.

This is where the name, or nature, of God, is revealed to Moses, I Am Who I Am. As I pointed out, this is not a name as we conceive of a name and that is because God is formless omnipresent potentiality, and a name as we conceive of a name is a way to compartmentalize and package a certain idea to understand it better, inherently imposing limitation upon it. But we cannot compartmentalize God, as 'he' is all life, and so the name of God is the statement of eternal presence and awareness of being, I AM WHO I AM. When we reflect on this omniscient living substance it reveals itself to us as I Am Who I Am, unlimited potentiality, presence, unformed, unconceptualized, pure awareness, oceanic information. We are the channels through which this I Am becomes known, we are the mirror God holds up to himself to see his own reflection, (image and likeness of God). Once we realize that the very essence of our being, our life, our I Am consciousness is Yahweh, we take on the responsibility of liberating our spiritual selves (Israelites) from the bondage of our primal animal instincts, our imprisonment to materiality (Egypt).

The Hebrew name for Egypt is Mizraim which means shut in, restraint, tribulation, distress, and represents our default nature as "slaves" to our carnal passions and desires which keeps us living in a base, adverse, dualistic state of being unable to consciously evolve. It is the duty of I Am to liberate the potentiality of our being for good and bring us into the land of milk and honey, Eden, the kingdom of God on earth.

Moses reached a certain state of enlightenment where he grasps the I Am on a universal scale and through it was able to liberate his people from material bondage, with this also came a higher set of law and order, namely the Ten Commandments. This led to an ethnocentric understanding of God and his universal laws but as we read in Exodus, once liberated and distinguished as their own race of people that were seeking to establish themselves, they came into opposition time and time again from every other race and tribe around them who also had their own set of beliefs and laws. And this is the state of religion and spiritual understanding humanity has been stuck in since then, thousands of years later. Which is strange living in a post-Jesus world, considering Jesus work was the same as Moses but instead of liberating one race of people he came to liberate all of humanity individually and intern the entire earth.

It states in Matthew 5:45 Jesus says, "That you may be sons of your Father in heaven; for He makes His sun rise on the evil and on the good and sends rain on the just and on the unjust." At all times Jehovah, I Am, is evolving out of the unified whole into duality and ultimately into the individualized conscious manifestation of the one being. We are the manifest presence of Jehovah, I Am. Unless we know that our being is, I Am, Jehovah, and live in the presence of him through our Christ consciousness, consciousness of Christ, and we shall always default back to our isolated, false self from which all sin is derived. "Therefore I said to you that you will die in your sins; for if you do not believe that I Am He, you will die in your sins," John 8:24. In this original passage the word, He, was not there, meaning this passage is supposed to be read as, "if you do not believe that I AM, you will die in your sins. "When we awaken to this, we realize it is a deathless principle, "will become in him a fountain of water springing up into everlasting life" John 4:14.

In Matthew 1:23, Jesus' name given to him is Emmanuel, which means God with or within us. Christ means anointed one, and Jesus Christ shows us the joining of the earthly Son of Man, Jesus, with the divine Son of God, Christ. Jesus is Greek for Yeshua, which means Jehovah saves, once again reminding us that unity, into duality, back into willful conscious unity, is the process through which we must be saved. "That if you confess with your mouth the Lord Jesus and believe in your heart that God has raised Him from the dead, you will be saved," Romans 10:9.

Jehovah is an infinite ocean of information, of meaning. Our souls are constellations of data suspended within the infinite informational lattice that is Jehovah, I AM. The story of the children of Israel is the story of truth vs falsity. Living from the consciousness of Christ, they align themselves with the omnipotence, omniscience and omnipresence of Jehovah, the formless God above all Gods. During these times, they are liberated, victorious through trials and on a steady path of upward causality, conscious unfoldment, and spiritual regeneration. However, time and time again, the nation of Israel comes under persecution from foreign forces. With this persecution, the Israelites adopt the gods and idols of their enemies into their own lives and so turn away from the knowledge of God's true nature, falling away from the remembrance of Jehovah's sovereignty and infinitude. Here are just a few scriptures warning about the dangers of idol worship, which will lead us to a clear understanding of the relation between the Old Testament God of punishment and wrath and Jesus' demonstration of the New Testament God of love and forgiveness.

Exodus 20:15, "And God spoke all these words, saying, "I am the Lord your God, who brought you out of the land of Egypt, out of the house of slavery. "You shall have no other gods before me. "You shall not make for yourself a carved image, or any likeness of anything that is in heaven above, or that is in the earth beneath, or that is in the water under the earth. You shall not bow down to them or serve them, for I, the Lord your God, am a jealous God, visiting the iniquity of the fathers on the children to the third and the fourth generation of those who hate me."

Leviticus 26:1 says, "You shall not make idols for yourselves or erect an image or pillar, and you shall not set up a figured stone in your land to bow down to it, for I am the Lord your God."

Isaiah 44:6-20, "All who fashion idols are nothing, and the things they delight in do not profit. Their witnesses neither see nor know that they may be put to shame. Who fashions a god or casts an idol that is profitable for nothing?"

Jeremiah 10:1-25, "Hear the word that the Lord speaks to you, O house of Israel. Thus says the Lord: "Learn not the way of the nations, nor be dismayed at the signs of the heavens because the nations are dismayed at them, for the customs of the peoples are vanity. A tree from the forest is cut down and worked with an axe by the hands of a craftsman. They decorate it with silver and gold; they fasten it with hammer and nails so that it cannot move. Their idols are like scarecrows in a cucumber field, and they cannot speak; they have to be carried, for they cannot walk. Do not be afraid of them, for they cannot do evil, neither is it in them to do good."

Corinthians 3:5, "Put to death therefore what is earthly in you: sexual immorality, impurity, passion, evil desire, and covetousness, which is idolatry."

In the Exodus passage of 20:15, we see some of the harsh

language being used against people who disobey God and once again wonder if he is so loving, why would he chase down and doom innocent children because their father worshiped idols. All it is saying is that if I, as a father, turn my back on God, universal law, and either bring my children up never training them in the laws of God, or worse, actively bring them up teaching them false beliefs about Gods nature, who and how he operates and what our relation is to God, then that child will grow up either ignorant or adverse to God and so will their child and most likely that child's child. As we have discussed in depth already, God is omnipresent and omnipotent and "nothing shall be able to separate us from the love of God" (Romans 8:39), so we either consciously align ourselves with the nature of God or we become adverse to the universal principles of life and suffer the consequence. We see a chain reaction through the generations of the father who would turn his back on God and worship idols, or things of the world, limitations of dualistic materiality. Proverbs 22:6 says, "Train up a child in the way he should go, and when he is old, he will not depart from it. "An examination of the story of Gideon is a great example of why the God of the Old Testament seems different from the God of the New.

Note On The Story Of Gideon

Judges 6: "The Israelites did evil in the eyes of the Lord, and for seven years he gave them into the hands of the Midianites. 2 Because the power of Midian was so oppressive, the Israelites prepared shelters for themselves in mountain clefts, caves and strongholds. 3 Whenever the Israelites planted their crops, the Midianites, Amalekites and other eastern peoples invaded the country. 4 They camped on the land and ruined the crops all the way to Gaza and did not spare a living thing for Israel, neither sheep nor cattle nor donkeys. 5 They came up with their livestock and their tents like swarms of locusts. It was impossible to count them or their camels; they invaded the land to ravage it. 6 Midian so impoverished the Israelites that they cried out to the Lord for help.

7 When the Israelites cried out to the Lord because of Midian, 8 he sent them a prophet, who said, "This is what the Lord, the God of Israel, says: I brought you up out of Egypt, out of the land of slavery. 9 I rescued you from the hand of the Egyptians. And I delivered you from the hand of all your oppressors; I drove them out before you and gave you their land. 10 I said to you, 'I am the Lord

"

your God; do not worship the gods of the Amorites, in whose land you live.' But you have not listened to me."

11 The angel of the Lord came and sat down under the oak in Ophrah that belonged to Joash the Abiezrite, where his son Gideon was threshing wheat in a winepress to keep it from the Midianites. 12 When the angel of the Lord appeared to Gideon, he said, "The Lord is with you, mighty warrior."

13 "Pardon me, my lord," Gideon replied, "but if the Lord is with us, why has all this happened to us? Where are all his wonders that our ancestors told us about when they said, 'Did not the Lord bring us up out of Egypt?' But now the Lord has abandoned us and given us into the hand of Midian." 14 The Lord turned to him and said, "Go in the strength you have and save Israel out of Midian's hand. Am I not sending you?" 15 "Pardon me, my lord," Gideon replied, "but how can I save Israel? My clan is the weakest in Manasseh, and I am the least in my family." 16 The Lord answered, "I will be with you, and you will strike down all the Midianites, leaving none alive." 17 Gideon replied, "If now I have found favor in your eyes, give me a sign that it is really you talking to me. 18 Please do not go away until I come back and bring my offering and set it before you." And the Lord said, "I will wait until you return." 19 Gideon went inside, prepared a young goat, and from an ephah of flour, he made bread without yeast. Putting the meat in a basket and its broth in a pot, he brought them out and offered them to him under the oak. 20 The angel of God said to him, "Take the meat and the unleavened bread, place them on this rock, and pour out the broth." And Gideon did so. 21 Then the angel of the Lord touched the meat and the unleavened bread with the tip of the staff that was in his hand. Fire flared from the rock, consuming the meat and the bread. And the angel of the Lord disappeared. 22 When Gideon realized that it was the angel of the Lord, he exclaimed, "Alas, Sovereign Lord! I have seen the angel of the Lord face to face!"

23 But the Lord said to him, "Peace! Do not be afraid. You are not going to die." 24 So Gideon built an altar to the Lord there and called it The Lord Is Peace. To this day, it stands in Ophrah of the Abiezrites. 25 That same night, the Lord said to him, "Take the second bull from your father's herd, the one seven years old. Tear down your father's altar to Baal and cut down the Asherah pole beside it. 26 Then build a proper kind of altar to the Lord your God on the top of this height. Using the wood of the Asherah pole that you cut down, offer the second bull as a burnt offering." 27 So Gideon took ten of his servants and did as the Lord told him. But because he was afraid of his family and the townspeople, he did it at night rather than in the daytime.

28 In the morning, when the people of the town got up, there was Baal's altar, demolished, with the Asherah pole beside it cut down and the second bull sacrificed on the newly built altar! 29 They asked each other, "Who did this?" When they carefully investigated, they were told, "Gideon, son of Joash, did it." 30 The people of the town demanded of Joash, "Bring out your son. He must die because he has broken down Baal's altar and cut down the Asherah pole beside it." 31 But Joash replied to the hostile crowd around him, "Are you going to plead Baal's cause? Are you trying to save him? Whoever fights for him shall be put to death by morning! If Baal really is a god, he can defend himself when someone breaks down his altar." 32 So because Gideon broke down Baal's altar, they gave him the name Jerub-Baal that day, saying, "Let Baal contend with him."

Rather than living in harmony with Jehovah, the universal life force, the Israelites made the choice to worship the gods of Midian. This decision to turn away from acknowledging spirit as the ultimate source of life has limited their perception of its boundless possibilities and has left them trapped in a constrictive state of consciousness, represented by the Midians. The Bible emphasizes that idols are created by human hands, symbolizing the idea that matter is lifeless while consciousness is alive. Whatever we focus our consciousness on will grow and manifest in our reality. As Jesus said, "In my Father's house are many mansions," implying that each individual embodies a state of consciousness just as an idol embodies the projection of our consciousness onto it, restricting our ability to perceive higher realities.

We first encounter Gideon threshing wheat in a winepress. Threshing wheat is the process of separating the edible grain from the stem, representing one's quest for inner understanding and spiritual growth. This is taking place in a winepress, which symbolizes the transformative and intoxicating effects of spiritual truth once internalized. Jesus himself compared wine to his own blood, signifying the spreading of this spiritual power throughout the world for anyone willing to receive it (John 6:54-56). When we consume this "new wine," or spiritual life force, we become spiritually reborn and dead to sin but alive in Christ (Romans 6:11).

Gideon was diligently seeking to understand this spiritual truth (in the secrecy of the winepress), working tirelessly to keep it hidden from the Midianites. In other words, he was the only Israelite who turned inward for guidance, following Jesus' advice to pray alone and in private (Matthew 6:6). He struggled and persevered to find a spiritual truth (wine) that would grant him strength (edible grain) and break him free from his oppressive state of consciousness (separating the grain from the stem, or root of the problem).

In the story of Gideon, we see similarities to Jacob's night of wrestling with the Angel of the Lord. The darkness of spiritual struggle gives way to the light of spiritual revelation. Gideon, after much seeking and contending with his state of consciousness, is visited by an Angel who declares him a mighty warrior for the Lord. This reveals that his daily battle with depression requires a warrior spirit, as he has been persistently seeking spiritual breakthroughs.

The Angel tasks Gideon to take a young goat, symbolizing stubbornness and rebellion, and unleavened bread, representing sincerity and truth. These are poured out under a rock, symbolizing humanity's limited understanding before spiritual regeneration. The broth, representing cleansing and renewal, is poured over them as well. All of this takes place under an oak tree, derived from the Hebrew word Ail or El, signifying strength and expansive movement.

To summarize, under the presence of Elohim (God), Gideon sacrifices his mental stronghold of rebellion through a humble heart and purges his limited understanding in order to receive spiritual truth. The Angel then consumes the offering with fire from their staff, symbolizing the all-consuming presence of God, which regenerates Gideon's state of being.

Now liberated and operating in alignment with God's life force, Gideon is instructed to tear down the idols of Baal and Asherah and build an altar using their wood. These pagan idols represent bondage to earthly desires and must be consumed by spiritual fire in order for one to be free from their oppression. As Gideon sacrifices a bull on this new altar, it represents taming the untamed chaotic power within ourselves through the refining fire of the Holy Spirit. Asherah was associated with lustful practices, symbolizing our bondage to earthly pleasures, which must also be consumed by spiritual fire for true liberation from material forces.

To unravel the intricate story of Gideon would require a tome in itself, but let us begin to peel back the layers and see the greater meaning behind it all. Jehovah, the Almighty God, is the embodiment of all things, the source from which everything flows. Yet when we create idols or limited images of God, we confine ourselves and hinder our growth and evolution along righteous paths. This is akin to setting up dams in a mighty river - it does not stop the flow of water but rather redirects it, causing floods and destruction. Idol worship, as seen in satanic thought, is like a dam that goes against the will of God, turning His divine power into a destructive force instead of one that builds up. Just as a river flows harmoniously within its banks, so too should our perceptions and beliefs align with the limitless potential of God's creation. But by creating false images or idols, we are building strongholds in our consciousness that limit our understanding and prevent us from worshipping the true source of life. Believing in an anthropomorphized God - one who is depicted as a human on a throne in the sky - is just another form of idol worship. It restricts our perception and separates us from the true essence of God as All in All. This leads us down a path of isolation and suffering, distancing ourselves from the ultimate truth and beauty that animates all things.

On The Tower Of Babel

Let us examine another example on this topic to hammer home the point that the Old Testament God is one and the same as the New Testament God. People from the Old Testament simply had a limited conception of God. As we stated before, before humanity can take the leap into complete Christ consciousness, Absolute Being, we had to evolve through various stages of conscious progression. First, the prepersonal, omniconsciousness, no sense of self-awareness, time or space, to fragmented, personal consciousness (our current state), to a universal understanding of God's omnipresence through I AM, to the complete individualization of I AM in humanity through the incarnation of Christ Jesus, the transpersonal. Whether in ignorance or knowingly, the Israelites misused their relation to God, who is life and love and through this adverse state, suffered the consequence of their own misuse of the one power.

Pretty much everyone has heard about the Tower of Babel. I have read comments online from atheists using the story of Babel to mock Christianity and prove how Ludacris the Bible is. Once again, it simply comes down to ignorance and incapacity to perceive the deeper truths contained within these stories. Let us read through the story and then dissect it.

Genesis 11:1-9, "Now the whole world had one language and a common speech. 2 As people moved eastward, they found a plain in Shinar and settled there. 3 They said to each other, "Come, let's make bricks and bake them thoroughly." They used brick instead of stone and tar for mortar. 4 Then they said, "Come, let us build ourselves a city, with a tower that reaches to the heavens, so that we may make a name for ourselves; otherwise, we will be scattered over the face of the whole earth." 5 But the Lord came down to see the city and the tower the people were building. 6 The Lord said, "If as one people speaking the same language, they have begun to do this, then nothing they plan to do will be impossible for them. 7 Come, let us go down and confuse their language so they will not understand each other." 8 So the Lord scattered them from there over all the earth, and they stopped building the city. 9 That is why it was called Babel because the Lord confused the language of the whole world there. From there, the Lord scattered them over the face of the whole earth."

Once again, every sentence and every word in the bible is rich with significance, so let us break down this story bit by bit to find the true meaning and relevance to the topic at hand. We read in the first verse that the whole earth was of one language and one speech, meaning all of humanity was in a state of unity, a certain symbiotic consciousness. It then goes on to say that they journeyed from the east and found a plain in Shinar. East in the bible always signifies the within, implying Oneness with God (Garden of Eden was Eastward). The name Shinar means two rivers, divided stream, wholly severed, for it is the land through which the rivers Tigris and Euphrates flow. We can read this as they moved away from unity and oneness into division, a divided state of mind and, therefore a lower state of being, as the highest point of consciousness is pure unity; the further we descend from it, the greater the multiplicity and division. No longer in touch with their source of being, they start making decisions out of their segregated states of mind, such as making bricks instead of stone and slime instead of mortar. Stone in the bible represents the foundation of truth, the Ten Commandments were written on stone tablets, it is our most literal and base understanding of truth from which a deeper and more subtle truth can be understood. Making bricks for stone means they have lost the truth of God and are now operating from their own false mortal perceptions of truth. They had slime for mortar. The word mortar in Hebrew is Maktesh, meaning pounding, mashing, crushing, which signifies the exchange, turning over and thinking out of ideas in mind. Mortar is made by cooking limestone and then mixing it with water. As we have seen before, water represents cleansing and mental potentiality, which, in this case, is based on the foundation of truth, stone. But they did not use mortar. They used slime, so instead of thinking from the place of truth, their ideas stemmed from what is at hand, weak and undefined substance.

They sought to raise their tower to heaven. Out of their own limited human perspective, they sought to raise themselves to the level of God. We see here again the Luciferic thought, that which out of self-love seeks to exalt itself above and tower over those it perceives itself separate from. This exaltation of self slowly gives birth to the idea that man is the source of all things, that all things stem from him, consciousness, willpower, life, and that somehow dead matter randomly came together to form an intelligent, self-aware mind. Again, stealing the glory from God and attributing it to himself, when in reality, man is completely ignorant of what consciousness is and an infinite amount of other fundamental things about our universe. In a Babel "civilization," a spiritual and psychological amnesia takes hold of our soul, and we forget the great unifying force of the universe and believe that everything just randomly happened and nothing has meaning. In the story, this results in the scattering of their tongues, "confusion of tongues," there was no longer a common understanding or language because the unifying source had been rejected, and the separated self, self-love, self-deification had overtaken their sense of unity. This led to each one not being able to understand their neighbor, and therefore the life of each one seemed like foolish babel to the other, ultimately bringing destruction.

A clear picture should by this point be forming in our minds about the relation of God to humanity and see that the God of the Old Testament God is not some cruel, vengeful, maleficent force that loves to punish, but is the God of love that Jesus taught us of. It is simply the consequences of our alignment with or misuse of, the universal principles of life that we either enjoy or suffer from. Unfortunately, we are seeing this division and separation greater than ever before. The deification of the separate self, self-love and self-worship is rampant in our societies, and this is precisely why we are seeing a rise in tribalism, paganism and witchcraft. People seem incapable of understanding one another. Since we have striped Christianity out of the West, we no longer have a common, unifying language based on selfless love, and now each person is fortifying themselves within their own separate self-identity. We are plunging further into fragmentation, detachment, and isolation, mainly impart due to the internet. If we look at the global web as an extension of humanity's mind, we can see that the internet is the manifestation of the schizophrenic state of consciousness. With no local or central, base truths to unify and build from, we are hyper-realizing our own personalities by only feeding on information that fortifies our already firmly established personal beliefs.

When Jesus was asked what the first two fundamental laws are, he responded, "Here O Israel; the Lord our God, the Lord is ONE: and thou shalt love the Lord thy God with all thy heart, with all thy soul, with all thy mind, and with all thy strength. The second is this, thy shalt love thy neighbor as thy self." These commandments are deceptively simple at first glance, but with a bit of analyzing we see a profound depth. Firstly, Jesus presses the fact that God is ONE. This is not saying that God is one and that creation is second, third or fourth, it is telling us that God is ONE, in all, through all, omniscient, omnipotent, omnipresent, all consuming. We are the individualization of this universal, all-consuming generation of life. And what we are to love is this individual relation to God. It is not telling us to love God, because God is not a separate concise construct we are able to project love onto, but God is life and love itself. Jesus tells us the way to do this is with all our heart, soul, mind and strength because it is through these channels that we experience God and God experiences himself in us.

Living from this perspective, we realize that we are not our own, but Gods, and the love of God pours through our heart, soul, and mind, giving us strength and life. We now operate in life from the love of the truth that we are one with God, and this abolishes all walls we may have erected around us that prevented us from living in symphony with God. In turn, because God is love, the love you feel for God is God himself fully present and abiding in you. The second is like this love our neighbor as ourselves because our neighbor is ourself. Each individual is simply a unique expression of the one humanity. Humanity is a divine idea in the mind of God, Jehovah, I AM, is this divine ideal, and we are the image and likeness of it. Each of us is a crystalized manifestation of this one I Am, but it is the same I Am that each one of us partakes in. When each of us lives from our I Am consciousness, our Christ consciousness, and we become one body, the body of Christ. As we have seen, humanity in its "fallen" state of consciousness (expulsion from Eden) has hardened its heart to this truth and so feels obscured from God and one another, but Jesus, the perfect embodiment of I Am,

Jehovah, literally killed this delusion of separation on the cross, and whether you believe it or not, fully unified all humanity back to its original I Am state, giving us access once more to the garden of Eden, heaven on earth and comprehension of our ONENESS with God. When Jesus tells us that the second is as the first, to love our neighbor as ourselves, we see that as he said, "I in them, and You in Me; that they may be made perfect in one" John 17:23, what he is saying is that if I love you, then you exist in me, and for you to love me means I exist in you, God is the source of all love, and therefore all is ONE in God.

The living principle of evolution is the universal law, and when progress along the lines of love and selflessness stops, retrogression begins. By removing Christianity from society, we are removing this very truth, and so the only natural course we can take after this is degeneration into division, Babel, and war with our neighbor, and so destruction becomes our lot. Humanity is a membrane covering this earth, and what happens to one happens to us all. "Assuredly, I say to you, inasmuch as you did it to one of the least of these My brethren, you did it to Me." Mathew 25:40. Let us not mistake this love for something that it is not, though. People in society today are parading around in the name of "love," but the fruits of their "love" are rotten. Instead of unifying, they breed more division and spread violence. "You will know them by their fruits. Do men gather grapes from thornbushes or figs from thistles?17Even so, every good tree bears good fruit, but a bad tree bears bad fruit," Matthew 7:16. Do not get it twisted as we have been discussing. Love of self is not true love; true love always gives birth to something new, always flows along the lines of evolution, and gives itself for the benefit of the whole. "Love is patient, love is kind. It does not envy, it does not boast, it is not proud. It does not dishonor others, it is not self-seeking, it is not easily angered, it keeps no record of wrongs. Love does not delight in evil but rejoices with the truth. It always protects, always trusts, always hopes, always perseveres," 1 Corinthians 13:4-7.

Thomas Merton sums it up quite well in his book No Man is an Island. "To consider persons and events and situations only in the light of their effect upon me is to live on the doorstep of hell. Selfishness is doomed to frustration, centered as it is upon a lie. To live exclusively for myself, I must make all things bend themselves to my will as if I were a god. But this is impossible. Is there any more cogent indication of my creaturehood than the insufficiency of my own will? For I cannot make the universe obey me. I cannot make other people conform to my own whims and fancies. I cannot make even my own body obey me. When I give it pleasure, it deceives my expectation and makes me suffer pain. When I give myself what I conceive to be freedom, I deceive myself and find that I am the prisoner of my own blindness and selfishness and insufficiency."

Just as we can use electricity to power an electric chair or fill our homes with light and warmth depending on our intention behind how we choose to wire it, so it is with the living originating life energy that is our Father God. "You have given him his heart's desire, And You have not withheld the request of his lips," Psalms 21:2. "Nor is He served by human hands, as though He needed anything, since He Himself gives to all people life and breath and all things," Acts 17:25. God is eternal and there is no turning back from this mighty river of life we have been place within. Through understanding, comprehending the teachings of Jesus Christ and applying them into our lives we begin to align ourselves with this unstoppable all-consuming life force instead of erecting temples, statues, idols which act as prison bars to our comprehension of the incomprehensible, Father God. In these early stages of the conscious evolution of humanity (Old Testament) we had a limited perception of God as Absolute Being and our individual relation with him, but through the life, teachings, miracles, crucifixion, resurrection and ascension of Jesus Christ (New Testament) we now have no excuse as to being able to grasp and understand the full potentiality of the human. Through the joining of Heaven to earth that was fully realized in the incarnation of Jesus Christ we are now the temples of the Holy Spirit. "Do you not know that your body is a temple of the Holy Spirit who is in you, whom you have from God, and that you are not your own?1 Corinthian 6:19. "What agreement has the temple of God with idols? For we are the temple of the living God; just as God said, "I will dwell in them and walk among them; And I will be their God, and they shall be My people," 2 Corinthian 6:16. As we transcend our current personal fractured conscious structure through our mind of Christ, purchased for us by Jesus Christ, realizing our unification with I AM, we merge into a fully individualized manifestation of the ONE omniconscious life which in turn unites all humanity back with the Garden of Eden where the tree of life resides. Instead of unconsciously living symbiotically with all creation, we are now fully realized, Christ Conscious, individualizations of Yahweh eating freely of the tree of life. No-longer experiencing God as adverse, detached, judgmental, but knowing that our life is his life, the many are one and the one is love. This is the destiny of humanity.

On Paganism And Witchcraft

In this age, we are seeing a mass surge of paganism and witchcraft. This is happening for a couple of reasons. People need to be spiritually filled. At the core of every human being, we are spiritual, we all deeply feel this, and unfortunately, a lot of people have not been able to get their fill of conventional Christianity. This sets them on a course to seek the sacred in other places. As Mircea Eliade puts it in his book, The Sacred and the Profane: The Nature of Religion, "It must be added at once that such a profane existence is never found in the pure state. To whatever degree he may have desacralized the world, the man who has made his choice in favor of a profane life never succeeds in completely doing away with religious behavior." This is a topic unto itself that we do not have time to fully discuss here. But implies that at our core, we are spiritual, religious people, and if we do not worship the one life-giving God, the God of truth and love, then we will worship falsity and deception, leading to suffering, confusion and death. Secondly, the propagandized media for decades have slowly and methodically mocked, ridiculed, fault found, and outright attacked the church and Christianity, and we are now experiencing the fruits of this, which is the eradication of

Christian principles from society. Generations are growing up with a disturbingly erroneous, contorted perception of what Christianity is. The media has been and continues to churn out show after show, movie after movie, song after song, promoting and praising paganistic philosophy and witchcraft.

So, what is a witch? Obviously, witches are not pointy-nosed, green-faced evil people that fly around on brooms cackling. Witchcraft is a very real belief system that anyone can easily learn if they search the internet or go to a local bookstore, and masses of people are doing exactly this. It correlates directly with this age of Babel we are living in. Here is a quick and basic breakdown of what paganism and witchcraft fundamentally are. Both are polytheistic religions, pantheisms that attribute gods to every aspect of life. For instance, in witchcraft, there is a god of nature. In Greek mythology this was Pan. There are gods littered throughout cities: gods of subways, gods of freeways, gods that rule over certain city blocks. In Greek mythology, we are familiar with the pantheon of the lustful god, Zeus, the war god. Ares, god of the sun, Apollo, god of fertility, Priapus and on and on. Witchcraft operates under the same belief that behind every element, there is a god or spiritual force that lords over it. Why would this be a bad thing? Let us take a simple example. If you are a witch living in the city and you live in a part of the city that is dangerous, then the way to solve this would be to do a ritual to appease the god that resides over that portion of the city to grant you safe passage. In ancient times, though people are more frequently practicing this nowadays, if you wanted to get pregnant, then you would do a ritual to appease the god of fertility in hopes that she would give you her blessing and you would get pregnant.

In the age of soulless information where we live unplugged from the real and plugged into a hyperreality, experienced through a simulacrum, where anything and everything is at our fingertips, what's stopping little Susie down the street from whipping up an emoji spell to make sure she aces her next exam? Where is the harm in that? God is not a vending machine. As we have seen in previous chapters, Yahweh, is a God of love, of relationship. Only when we see ourselves as distinct, detached, separate entities do we feel that we need to coerce the forces that be to bend to our bidding. This is ultimately an ego-driven, false self-exalting, and therefore Luciferic state of being that will always lead to suffering. Even when using supposed white magic, we are still imposing our will, the will of the personal self, over the will of the whole, the holy will, and therefore interfering with a chain of events in someone else's life that we know nothing about. Do you know what started your heart beating? Do you know where your next thought comes from? Then why would we assume we know what is best for someone else, more so than God?

In a belief system that sees spirits, elementals, gods and the like operating and lording over their designated territory comes a great psychological imbalance. If I accept this as my belief, then I have suddenly spun an ensnaring web for myself where I am constantly trying to appease various forces that may have maleficent will toward me if I do not do the right ritual, spell, or incantation. Instead of living from the truth that there is one power, one source, which I am united with, which is love, I live in constant flux, being pulled this way and that between forces that could get out of hand if not properly acknowledged and appeased. Unity brings harmony; only through harmony can we have a truly functioning civilization.

Another component to this is the one everyone is familiar with, which is casting spells, writing and activating sigils, invocations, and incantations. All these practices come from the assertion of one's selfish will. If I feel the need to formulate some ritual in order to sway the universe one way or another, then I am operating from the standpoint of the Luciferic, the belief that I, the created, know better than the creator. I am raising my tower of brick and slime to heaven to deify myself through force.

Historically, witchcraft has been associated with women, and there is a good reason for this. Women throughout most societies have been unjustly oppressed by men and so thirst to take back some semblance of power. This stems from what Carl Jung called the hunger for power. "The individual's feeling of weakness, indeed of non-existence, [is] compensated by the eruption of hitherto unknown desires for power (Carl Jung, The Fight with the Shadow). Witchcraft is the personal, virtual self's yearning to reclaim control and dominance of its life. Once again, it all stems from the erroneous belief of the separate self and the assertion of the will of this false self.

There is a story in the book of Acts of the Apostles 8:9-24, which tells us of a sorcerer who sought the power of the Holy Spirit. "Now, for some time, a man named Simon had practiced sorcery in the city and amazed all the people of Samaria. He boasted that he was someone great, and all the people, both high and low, gave him their attention and exclaimed, "This man is rightly called the Great Power of God." They followed him because he had amazed them for a long time with his sorcery. But when they believed Philip as he proclaimed the good news of the kingdom of God and the name of Jesus Christ, they were baptized, both men and women. Simon himself believed and was baptized. And he followed Philip everywhere, astonished by the great signs and miracles he saw.

When the apostles in Jerusalem heard that Samaria had accepted the word of God, they sent Peter and John to Samaria. When they arrived, they prayed for the new believers there that they might receive the Holy Spirit because the Holy Spirit had not yet come on any of them; they had simply been baptized in the name of the Lord Jesus. Then Peter and John placed their hands on them, and they received the Holy Spirit. When Simon saw that the Spirit was given at the laying on of the apostles' hands, he offered them money and said, "Give me also this ability so that everyone on whom I lay my hands may receive the Holy Spirit." Peter answered: "May your money perish with you because you thought you could buy the gift of God with money! You have no part or share in this ministry because your heart is not right before God. Repent of this wickedness and pray to the Lord in the hope that he may forgive you for having such a thought in your heart. For I see that you are full of bitterness and captive to sin." Then Simon answered, "Pray to the Lord for me so that nothing you have said may happen to me."

Before Simon, the sorcerer, received the Holy Spirit and he was doing signs and wonders that amazed the people. But if he did not have the Holy Spirit, then from what source did he draw his power? As we have gone over in length if the devil and evil are absolute opposites of God and God is the source of all life and creativity, then the devil and evil have no power to create anything, and if Simon was not operating in alignment with the will of God as he did not have the Holy Spirit at this time, he must of being using the ONE power of God adversely. And when we read this scripture, we find exactly this.

It says that "he boasted that he was someone great," here again, we find the Luciferic thought that sets itself up in opposition to God by attributing all power and creativity to their virtual self instead of the true originating living substance of God. Notice Philip and John do great signs and wonders demonstrating great power, but they attribute it to God and Jesus Christ, never themselves. They attribute it to Jesus Christ because he is the first in the new race of spiritually alive, regenerated humanity operating in unity with God. In the name of Jesus Christ, we find the universal (Christ) married to the personal (Jesus), and this signifies the final and complete unification of Heaven with earth, God inseparably ONE with humanity. This is why all things must be done in the 'name' of Jesus Christ. It is not the name 'Jesus' itself that has the power, if this were the case, then every Spanish-speaking family with a member named Heyzeus would be walking around accidently raising people from the dead. No, the power is in the understanding of what the name represents. That we are no-longer subject and victim to random circumstances and situations of this earth, gross matter is no-longer dominant over us, but all things in our life are returned to the divine design of spiritual power over the physical manifest universe in and through the body of Jesus Christ. "The power of death was over all men because of the sin of one man, Adam. But many people will receive His loving-favor and the gift of being made right with God. They will have power in life by Jesus Christ," (Romans 5:17). "Ye are of God, little children, and have overcome them: because greater is he that is in you, than he that is in the world," (1 John 4:4). "And I will give you the keys of the kingdom of heaven, and whatever you bind on earth will be bound in heaven, and whatever you loose on earth will be loosed in heaven" Matthew 16:19.

This is where our power lies, in the right understanding of where our source originates, the marriage of Almighty God with the individual, firstly and rightly demonstrated by Jesus Christ. Simon the Sorcerer saw this power and wanted to gain it so he could use it to win the applause of the people. Offering Philip and John money for it is telling us that he is still locked in the material consciousness and therefore unable to wake up to the truth of the spirit, that we do not own it, it is not something that can be bought or possessed but it is something that we awaken within and realize that it already is us. This is why it is a 'gift' from God. The same attitude of Simon is the same as the practitioner of witchcraft or Paganism. How many blood sacrifices to the multiple gods have been made over the years trying to buy the favor of the gods with material offerings, or Charon's obol placed in the mouth of the deceased to pay off

Charon the ferryman for safe passage over the river Styx. This all comes from the perspective of material dominance over the spiritual and therefore keeps us bound by limitation, locked outside of the Garden of Eden and in the Labyrinth of our own personal mind where a mutated beast lies in wait at its core (our fallen nature). As Peter demonstrated in Acts 3:6, "Silver and gold I do not have, but what I do have I give you: In the name of Jesus Christ of Nazareth, rise up and walk." The gift of the Holy Spirit is free for us all to realize, but we do not own or possess it. In truth, nothing in this life belongs to us, it is all freely given to us and we are simply partaking of it, even 'your' body. "The earth is the LORD's, and everything in it. The world and all its people belong to him," Psalm 24:1.

Believing we can concoct and combine certain elements together to influence a certain spiritual outcome is a complete abomination and disrespect toward God, who has based the entire universe off relationship and love. We cannot coerce the All-Knowing, Ever-Living, Self-Existent one on, by throwing some herbs together, lighting a few candles and sending out 'good vibes.' This is only what a spiritually deaf, dumb and blind person would believe. But do not worry. Jesus came to set the captives free and give sight to the blind. We need to stop thinking that God is some completely separate entity that must be strongarmed into doing the bidding of our personal self. This is why witchcraft and paganism are so offensive to God because it is an insult to his very nature, that of love and relationship, not force and manipulation.

Without an Axis Mundi, a centralization and establishing of universal truth known through the spirit of truth, humanity will collapse. As Jesus states in Mathew 12:25, "Every kingdom divided against itself is brought to desolation, and every city or house divided against itself will not stand."

As we have seen with the Tower of Babel, without a common language (understanding of the universal principles of life) civilization becomes unbalanced and collapses. There is power in ritual when ritual is done with a heightened awareness of the inner spiritual significance of the actions. But ritual must always be done in worship, reverence to God, and not in an act of coercion to receive the gratification of one's selfish will as is the case with Magick or Paganism. As Jesus showed us that " not my will but thine be done," not the personal will but the universal will, the whole will be done, not for my selfish gratification and glory but for the good of all humanity. With paganism and witchcraft, we inevitably revert back to tribalism, Babel, division, isolation, and fortification in the false self. Therefore, paganism and witchcraft ultimately were not and will not be able to stand for the long term on a mass scale. Unfortunately, it looks like Western societies will fall back into paganism and witchcraft once again. But without an axis, a centralizing coherent truth that only comes from a death of selfish desire and selfless alignment with the spirit of Christ within every individual, it will eventually destroy itself as it has done in the past through division which is inherently at its core. This will, thankfully however, make way for a renaissance of ONENESS once we have evolved past this period of spiritual Dark Age that is upon us.

WHO IS SATAN
(FROM A BIBLICAL PERSPECTIVE)

Satan, the devil, what a subject of fascination that people have been captivated with for thousands of years. Books, art, literature, religions, movies, TV shows, and music have all taken this subject of the devil and used it to enthrall, empower, entertain and blame over the centuries. But what exactly is the devil, and what does the bible honestly say about the devil? First off, the devil in pop culture we have become familiar with does not exist in the bible. The horned, pitch-fork wielding devil was popularized in images used in Dante's Devine Comedy and by the end of the Middle Ages this image had taken hold in the imaginations of humanity. The Hebrew sages who wrote the Bible did not conceive of the 'devil' as we do. Instead, they have the figure Satan who, instead of an independent agent who has his own sweet little abode in hell, is a figure that works with the power of Jehovah, as in the book of Job, for instance. But the devil, as we have come to know it, is never described in detail in the bible, and there is a good reason for this.

We need to go back to the origins of what becomes known as the devil and, eventually, the Great Red Dragon of revelation to get a clear picture of the biblical archetype known as the devil. We have already gone through Genesis three, where we discover the first account of Satan, who is represented as a serpent. How do we know this serpent is the same as Satan and the devil? Because in the book of Revelation, St. John tells us that they are all one and the same, in Revelation 20:2, "He laid hold of the dragon, that serpent of old, who is the Devil and Satan, and bound him for a thousand years." In the New King James interpretation and others, the word "the" is italicized. This is because "the" was not in the original text. Why is this important? Because it indicates a personal being, but this indication of a solo being is not in the original scripture. To better understand this, we need to understand what the names Satan and Devil mean. In the original Hebrew, Satan means liar, adversary, accuser, the name Devil means the same thing. This tells us that every time we read the name of Satan or the Devil, we are to read it as an adversary, liar, or accuser. So how can the little, subtle serpent be the same evil force as Satan? Let us look again at Genesis three to get a clearer picture.

3Now, the serpent was more subtle than any other wild creature that Jehovah had made. He said to the woman, "Did God say, 'You shall not eat of any tree of the garden?" And the woman said to the serpent, "We may eat of the fruit of the trees of the garden; but God said, 'You shall not eat of the fruit of the tree, which is the midst of the garden, neither shall you touch it, lest you die." But the serpent said to the woman, "You will not die. For God knows that when you eat of it, your eyes will be opened, and you will be like God, knowing good and evil." So, when the woman saw that the tree was good for food and that it was a delight to the eyes, and that the tree was to be desired to make one wise, she took of its fruit and ate; and she also gave some to her husband, and he ate. Then the eyes of both were opened, and they knew that they were naked, and they sewed fig leaves together and made themselves aprons."

We have gone over this in the first chapters of this book, but let us look again at a few key things. It says that the serpent was more subtle than any other creature. Some definitions of subtle are capable of making fine distinctions, delicately complex and understated. We should remember that the Garden of Eden is the soul, and Adam and Eve are one being at this point and all they know is God, good. Jehovah is diversifying and unfolding the divine ideals set forth by Elohim, and as these ideals in the divine mind get worked out, they go through the process of crystallization into denser and denser forms. Eve represents the feeling, and emotional nature of the soul, so right after she is formed, the serpent is mentioned. The serpent is the next natural product after the feeling, sensation-soul is formed as it is the linking connection between soul-sensation and elemental life. When we read the bible, we find no story of how the devil was created, there is the story about Lucifer and we will go over that in the next video, but as far as the bible saying, "and God created the devil," it is not to be found anywhere! And so, we find that the genesis of the devil starts off from this subtle serpent who represent the inversion of truth, of knowing good, God as the source and first cause of all, the ONE life from which all things take their form, to, believing that the formed is a life of its own that can satisfy the soul. This whole drama takes place around the tree of the knowledge of good and evil, which is the knowledge of the right relation between spirit as first cause and elemental life as effect. But the serpent, whose purpose is sensatory function, is to relay and communicate to our feeling nature, information about the elemental world so we can continue to express and expand our experience.

And we can see that this is the case when we study Exodus 21:4-9, where Moses lifts up a bronze serpent and Jesus referred to himself as a serpent that must be lifted up. Jesus was the son of God and therefore cannot be the devil who is associated with the serpent, so clearly this serpent in Exodus and what Jesus spoke of is referring to something that was originally created by God and all things created by God are good. It is only after the appropriation of evil from the tree that this serpent is associated with evil.

One of the curses Jehovah gives this serpent is that it crawls on its belly, so we can assume that its original position was upright, signifying that it is in alignment with Jehovah as we always use the vertical line as a symbol of divine ascent and descent. This serpent, sense consciousness, relays to Eve that this tree of good and evil looks delicious, and good for food, she begins to perceive the manifest, elemental substance as a substance that contains life within itself. This is the great deception. She begins to perceive that evil, detachment from God, is something that has life within itself. Her perception of the created has subtly shifted to perceive it as having life in and of itself and this is universally false, Satan is the father of lies. She takes this knowledge of evil into herself, this inversion of the truth, which is that evil is a power in itself that is to be known, and because her and Adam are one being at this time, he too takes this false knowledge into himself, and then the serpent immediately accuses them of being naked. Naked meaning, they are now aware of a separation between them and all other things. At first, themselves and the entire cosmos were one unified integral entity, now they are spatially aware of themselves as isolated entities distinct from the earth, "they were ashamed." Hopefully, a clearer picture is beginning to form in your mind of what Satan, the accuser is.

What Is Evil

(According to the Bible)

We can safely say that God and the devil are absolute opposites. God is all life; therefore, the devil is no life, therefore God exists, and the devil does not. But how can this thing that does not exist occupy so much of our culture and even space in the Bible. If we turn on the news or read history, it is undeniable that a force of evil exists. We know that for life to be, it must be creative and affirmative, which are the very attributes of God, "in the beginning God created," if the devil is opposite of this, then there is no creative power in the devil and renders itself null and void immediately. This means there can be no universal power of evil that has its own kingdom.

The Bible is explicit in stating that there is only ONE power, and this power is most high, Almighty, self-existent, ever-living. If there is only one power, one source from which all things "live, move, and have their being within," Acts 17:28, then we need to realize that evil is simply the inversion of the one power. Take cancer, for example. Cancer is the breakdown of the orderly process of cell creation in the body. The human body is made up of trillions of cells, which grow, divide and form new cells as the body needs them. New cells continue to form when the old, abnormal or damaged cells that are no longer needed have still not died. These abnormal cells join together into tumors. These tumors are malignant and destroy the body from the inside out. The takeaway from this is that the disease of cancer is caused by disharmony, a form of chaos, a breakaway from the orderly unified system of relationships that the body is built on. The malignant tumors are created from cells that the body naturally produces. This detachment from the systematic order causes the eventual death of its host. The exact same can be said of evil and how it is formed. Eden was the systemic integral order of the relationship between all things, Adam and Eve existing in a symbiotic unconscious state. Once we took into ourselves, ate of the fruit, the knowledge that evil is a power and force unto itself, we detached ourselves from the one true life force of all creation, God. As cancer forms tumors, we formed a false self, a virtual self, which closes itself off from the omnipresent flow of God's presence. Just as malignant tumors invade and toxify nearby tissue because they are now a foreign body birthed from the system they are destroying, so we, through the belief that evil is a force unto itself, take the One life power of God and turn it in on itself and use it to attack and destroy all that is not like it. Let us look at how Jesus tackled this force of inversion, this delusion of the virtual self and its lust to conquer all that is not of itself.

We read in Matthew 4:1, "1 Then Jesus was led by the Spirit into the wilderness to be tempted by the devil. 2 After fasting forty days and forty nights, He was hungry. 3 The tempter came to Him and said, "If You are the Son of God, tell these stones to become bread." 4 But Jesus answered, "It is written: 'Man shall not live on bread alone, but on every word that comes from the mouth of God." 5 Then the devil took Him to the holy city and set Him on the pinnacle of the temple. 6 "If You are the Son of God," he said, "throw Yourself down. For it is written: 'He will command His angels concerning You, and they will lift You up in their hands, so that You will not strike Your foot against a stone." 7 Jesus replied, "It is also written: 'Do not put the Lord your God to the test." 8 Again, the devil took Him to a very high mountain and showed Him all the kingdoms of the world and their glory. 9 "All this I will give You," he said, "if You will fall down and worship me." 10 "Away from Me, Satan!" Jesus declared. "For it is written: 'Worship the Lord your God and serve Him only." 11 Then the devil left Him, and angels came and ministered to Him.

To properly understand what is going on here, we need to see the evolution of human consciousness holistically. The creation story of Eden and that of Adam and Eve is a prepersonal state of being. Jehovah, all the animals, Adam and Eve, all exist in a symbiotic state of complete union, and they did not know they were naked. In other words, Adam and Eve could not tell the difference between themselves, the plants, animals, trees, skies and earth, and all was whole. We strangely assume that our ancestor's state of awareness was similar to our own, but if we look at cave paintings, or beliefs in magic and animism, we can see that their state of awareness was intrinsically linked to their surroundings, so much so that they could not distinguish where the world ended and they began. No objective sense of time or space. With the assimilation of the knowledge that evil, or that which is absolute opposite and other than God, occurred, a personal, fragmented state of being was formed. An individuality, time and space as a construct, a spatialized consciousness, awakened within us. Now, our world within and the world without begin to detach, fragment, and meaning only exists within us and not out there. Our consciousness becomes fragmented, and our perspective of reality narrows. This segmented state of mind causes us to lose sight of the whole, which is caused by the rational mind (Cain) compartmentalizing and dissecting all things through its estranged relation to reality as a whole and objectifying space and time. The entangled web of integral relationships of Eden begins to unravel, and we relate to the cosmos as a foreign entity that needs to be measured, objectified, controlled and manipulated. This is Cain killing Abel and building the first city. This detachment from omni-being, into personal being is a necessary step in Jehovah's grand plan, as his desire for us is to be individualized, free-willed beings who consciously and willfully return to paradisical Eden (manifest the kingdom of heaven within). So, this non-dualistic state of being, Adam/Eve, though unified with Jehovah in Eden, was experienced as a spaceless, timeless, pretemporal paradise with Adam and Eve not knowing they were naked, not having an individualized conscious perspective, in other words, they were unconscious. For us to progress to a state of conscious union with God, a stage of detachment from our intrinsic relation with the cosmos had to occur, and this is summed up with what Jehovah tells Cain in Genesis 4:12. "When you till the ground, it shall no longer yield its strength to you. A fugitive and a vagabond you shall be on the earth." This tells us that the symbiotic conscious relation Adam, Eve, and Cain had with the cosmos is now fractured, and instead of a non-personal relation to all things, a severing of the umbilical cord with the womb of creation has occurred. Humanity, represented through Cain, is still in the unconscious sleep of Adam, as the fractured consciousness, the virtual self, can only perceive a very limited frame of reality. When our perception of the real is narrow,4particular, and therefore fragmented, we are unaware of reality as a whole and so in a state of unconsciousness.

Humanity from here begins their long and slow process of gradual conscious awakening until a breakthrough occurs with Moses at the burning bush when he has the revelation that the name, essence, and presence of God is I AM. This is a jolt that awakens within Moses our right relation to God that God is the very presence that we perceive as 'our' life. This evolution of consciousness had occurred within individuals before this, as what happened in the famous story of Jacobs's ladder, but Moses is tasked with giving the key to this conscious evolution to the masses and forming the first great collective of individuals that are unified under the knowledge of I AM. This is the importance of the Israelites, carriers of the true identity of I Am, Jehovah, and humanity's relation to him. The Israelites begin to strive toward a transpersonal experience of being. Knowing that each one is an individualization of the omnipresent, omniscient, omnipotent God Jehovah, but also collectively, they are the people of the I AM. This is why they were the first to do away with idol worship and pagan rituals as they were awake within, able to transcend their personal state of being, which is what the anthropomorphizing of gods is a product of. No longer unconscious, no longer detached and personal, but moving toward an individualized understanding of the transpersonal, symbiotic cosmic relation to the whole. The Old Testament portion of the Bible, from the point of Exodus, takes us through the struggle, success and failure of the integration of this omni-consciousness into humanity. Then along comes Jesus Christ. The God-man whose mission it was to take humanity by the hand and usher in the new eon of enlightenment by demonstrating what the reality of this transpersonal, omni-conscious state of being looks like on an individual scale. Here, we pick up where we began with the temptation of Christ. In order for Jesus to synthesize heaven with earth once more globally and do away with the objective, detached, mechanical, human perspective of the universe, he must demonstrate it in himself first.

As we have seen, Satan developed out of the inversion of the function of the serpent, which is now the agent whose job it is to accuse and be adverse to all things. Without this accusation, Adam and Eve would never have known that they were naked, would never have develop a detached, separate self-identity and therefore would have never perceived themselves as leaving the presence of Jehovah, the garden of Eden. This accusation that we are naked, we are detached from all things, carried through all the way up until Jesus' time. The true knowledge of God's identity as I AM, which is his presence, was lost and those in religious positions who were supposed to be keepers of this knowledge had lost sight of it themselves. Jesus comes against the Scribes and Pharisees in Matthew 23, in the passage of the seven woes, where he scolds them for hoarding spiritual knowledge and for shutting up the kingdom of heaven so no one may know its reality. To unleash the spirit of Christ upon the earth and raise humanity to Christ's consciousness Jesus must face the accusation of the accuser, that within him which would try to convince him that he is detached and isolated from God.

The number four in the bible stands for that which is created, effect, not cause. The account of Jesus being tempted in Matthew and Luke both take place in chapter four, meaning this is Jesus' trial of earthly temptation to take the way of the world and not the way of the spirit. To take the created as the first cause and fall into the delusion of separation, his temptation to eat of the tree of the knowledge of evil. He is filled with the Holy Spirit, the presence of Jehovah, and he then goes to the wilderness. Wilderness represents the estranged and adverse relation humanity has with the world in its current objectifiable, mechanical, personal consciousness.

Forty days and forty nights represent the completeness, equal on all sides, foursquare, of spiritual supremacy over matter. The devil now comes to tempt Jesus now that he is in a physically drained and hungered state. The Holy Spirit is the tangible presence of our awareness of our unity with God, which keeps us in a loving, selfless, symbiotic state of consciousness, Christ onsciousness. However, Jesus was both the Son of God and the Son of Man. Meaning there was the Jesus Christ part of him, which is the true self, the image and likeness of God. And there was the Jesus of Nazareth, the Carpenter's son, part of him which is the virtual self, the personal self that we have been discussing. We see Jesus struggle with this personal side of himself mainly twice in scripture, once in this account of the temptation, the other in the account of the night before his crucifixion in the garden of Gethsemane. Jesus' mission here is to individually overcome the prepersonal and personal states of consciousness that have kept humanity shrouded in darkness and turn his awareness into the transpersonal, which unifies the lower states into the omni-consciousness of Jehovah. Satan, the accuser, the tempter, the adversary, comes and tells Jesus, "turn these stones to bread." In response, Jesus simply turns his carnal mind, Jesus of Nazareth mind, away from the thought of material satisfaction and recites the truth of spirit, "Man shall not live on bread alone, but on every word that comes from the mouth of God." He is setting in his mind the right relation between spirit and matter, we shall live from the word of God first, the spiritual substance of God shall fill us and satisfy us first, and then we eat of the material bread. The exact opposite of what Eve did in the Garden of Eden, seeking substance from the fruit over substance from God.

Next, he is taken to the pinnacle of the temple. Notice he is on top of the temple at the pinnacle, on the exterior. Jesus' entire mission was to demonstrate that our body is the temple of God, not an outer building. This points us to the fact that these temptations are coming from the carnal mind, the personal private state of consciousness that seeks to use and manipulate the one universal power of God for its own selfish gain. The accuser tells him to throw himself off the temple, and God will surely catch him. Jesus dissolves this thought of personal glory once again with the truth that we do not put God to the test, meaning when we live in complete unity with God, there is no conflict between the will of the personal and the will of the whole because we understand that we are an individualization of Jehovah, I AM. We would only need to test God if our conception of God is erroneous and God is perceived as something other and unknowable from ourselves. Jesus knew that God's will is his will, and therefore, whatever he did, he did through God, which renders testing God completely pointless. As Jesus said himself later, "I can do nothing on My own initiative. As I hear, I judge; and My judgment is just, because I do not seek My own will, but the will of Him who sent Me," John 5:30.

The third and final accusation comes in the form of dominance over all earthly kingdoms. Fast forward to the book of Revelation and we see that St. John is also carried away in the spirit to the wilderness and sees the personification of the fallen state of humanity in a slightly different way.

Revelation 17:3, 3 So he carried me away in the spirit into a wilderness, and I saw a woman sitting on a scarlet beast that was full of blasphemous names, and it had seven heads and ten horns. 4 The woman was clothed in purple and scarlet, and adorned with gold and jewels and pearls, holding in her hand a golden cup full of abominations and the impurities of her fornication; 5 and on her forehead was written a name, a mystery: 'Babylon the great, mother of whores and of earth's abominations.' 6 And I saw that the woman was drunk with the blood of the saints and the blood of the witnesses to Jesus.

We see here a graphic image of the fallen race mind where all the kingdoms of the world are personified as the whore of Babylon. We do not have time to go into depth about all the symbolism described here, but this is what the glory of the kingdoms of the world can be summed up as, and Jesus obviously does not want any part of that. The whore of Babylon is the epitome of the worship of the self, the lusting after all things of the objectified world and the exaltation of the created over the creator. This Satanic thought (thought adverse to the truth that God is the first cause) of ruling over people through force, material power, and glory tempts Jesus, but in order to attain it, Jesus must "fall down and worship" Satan. Meaning

Jesus must deny his Christ identity, which is the image and likeness of God, omni-conscious, and must use the life power of Jehovah for self-glorification, which would lead to a falling down or falling away from the presence of God and into a dualistic delusion, just as the serpent had to crawl on his belly. Jesus declares, "away from me, Satan," or in other words, away from me that which is a false perception. And immediately fills his mind with the truth that we shall worship Jehovah, the ONE, and worship him only. Jesus acknowledges that Jehovah is the ONE life and ONE power. When we live in the conscious awareness of this truth, evil, Satan, the lie, naturally dissolves into its native nothingness. After he combats the delusional thoughts of personal glorification, angels come and minister to him, meaning divine ideas once more flood his awareness, and he has successfully synthesized with his Christ consciousness and is therefore ready to begin his ministry.

Is Lucifer Satan?

So, if evil is no-thing, and Satan is the inversion and perversion of the ONE power, then what about Lucifer? Again, so much has been adlibbed about Lucifer in cultures throughout the ages that we are suffering from a type of Mandela Effect. If we actually look at the original source and take only what the bible, the inspired word of God, says, then we find that it actually says very little.

The figure of Lucifer is only written about specifically once in the bible, in Isaiah 14, and potentially twice. The second account does not specifically naming the figure spoken of as Lucifer, but the essence of the figure is close to what Isaiah describes. In both accounts these prophets are tasked with chastising a very real king and his kingdom. Isaiah is tasked with scolding the king of Babylon, and Ezekiel is tasked with scolding the king of Tyre.

The name Lucifer means shining one, light-bearer. In King James' interpretation of the Latin text, Venus is the day star and morning star. In 2 Peter 1:19, Jesus Christ is referred to as the morning star, "as a light that shines in a dark place, until the day dawns and the morning star rises in your hearts." How can it be that

Satan, Lucifer, and Jesus Christ are both referred to as the morning star, is this not absolute blasphemy?

Let us first take a look at the direct account Isaiah gives. Both Isiah and Ezekiel's accounts start off with their reproach directed at the king themselves, then suddenly, halfway through this scolding of the figure of the king, they switch and start talking about a type of angelic being who, out of pride, fell from the graces of God, then switch back to scolding the king's kingdom and prophecy that it will fall. Here in lies a great clue to what Lucifer actually is. Let us read through the specific account that Isaiah gives, directly referring to this being as Lucifer. We will lead in with the opening passages to get the full context.

Isaiah 14, "For the Lord will have mercy on Jacob, and will yet choose Israel, and set them in their own land: and the strangers shall be joined with them, and they shall cleave to the house of Jacob. And the people shall take them, and bring them to their place: and the house of Israel shall possess them in the land of the Lord for servants and handmaids: and they shall take them captives, whose captives they were; and they shall rule over their oppressors. And it shall come to pass in the day that the Lord shall give thee rest from thy sorrow, and from thy fear, and from the hard bondage wherein thou wasn't made to serve, That thou shalt take up this proverb against the king of Babylon, and say, How hath the oppressor ceased! The golden city ceased! The Lord hath broken the staff of the wicked, and the scepter of the rulers. He who smote the people in wrath with a continual stroke, he that ruled the nations in anger is persecuted, and none hindereth. The whole earth is at rest and is quiet: they break forth into singing.

[12]How art thou fallen from heaven, O Lucifer, son of the morning! How art thou cut down to the ground, which didst weaken the nations![13]For thou hast said in thine heart, I will ascend into heaven, I will exalt my throne above the stars of God: I will sit also upon the

mount of the congregation, in the sides of the north:[14]I will ascend above the heights of the clouds; I will be like the most High.[15]Yet thou shalt be brought down to hell, to the sides of the pit.[16]They that see thee shall narrowly look upon thee, and consider thee, saying, Is this the man that made the earth to tremble, that did shake kingdoms;[17]That made the world as a wilderness, and destroyed the cities thereof; that opened not the house of his prisoners?[18]All the kings of the nations, even all of them, lie in glory, every one in his own house.[19]But thou art cast out of thy grave like an abominable branch, and as the raiment of those that are slain, thrust through with a sword, that go down to the stones of the pit; as a carcass trodden under feet.[20]Thou shalt not be joined with them in burial, because thou hast destroyed thy land, and slain thy people: the seed of evildoers shall never be renowned."

In scripture, Babylon has always represented material dominance, and the inhabitants of Babylon worship the material, the deification of the virtual self, as we saw with the passage from Revelation. The king of Babylon, the pinnacle of this ideology, stands for the personification of this inversion by attributing to the personal self the qualities of God. This is the Luciferic mind state. Notice, Isaiah when speaking from Lucifer's perspective, keeps saying, "I will," and then in verse 16 calls him a man, "Is this the man that made the earth to tremble." Isiah is writing from the perspective of the king's prideful mind state of self-worship, hence calling him a man. As Jesus demonstrated in the garden of Gethsemane, our state of being should always be, "thy will, not my will be done," because when operating from omni-consciousness, our mind of Christ, we are operating in the will of the whole and our own personal self, the virtual self, understands its place as simply a vehicle which carries out the divine intent.

Over the years, people have merged a few pieces of scripture together to flesh out a bigger picture of this Lucifer character. They take this passage from Isaiah 12 and blend it with the passage from Revelation 12:7-9, "Then war broke out in heaven. Michael and his angels fought against the dragon, and the dragon and his angels fought back. 8 But he was not strong enough, and they lost their place in heaven. 9 The great dragon was hurled down—that ancient serpent called the devil, or Satan, who leads the whole world astray. He was hurled to the earth, and his angels with him."

Remember that the serpent is sense consciousness, that which consumes the dust of the earth, what the bible states our body is made from. The serpent is that which puts the created dominant over the creator, just as Lucifer exalts selfish will over the whole. This serpent from Genesis, over the millennia of human history, has grown and morphed into the great red dragon of Revelation. The human race is one family, and erroneous thoughts and beliefs compound themselves from generation to generation. The false thoughts and beliefs that the personal self has generated over the millennia have built on one another, and this is why we are seeing the collective effort to extinguish the light of spirit and exalt the material universe as the first cause and creator of all. Collectively and individually, this dragon, exalted false self, will go to war against our true identity as the image and likeness of God, our Christ self, but that which is false cannot stand in the light of the real and, therefore will be cast out of heaven as it is said will happen to the dragon. To shine more light on the fact that these forces, Satanic, Luciferic and the dragon, are not independent material forces but symbols of the states of consciousness the human race must transcend, we just need to listen to the words of Jesus himself, which gives us grounding for all that is being said. Luke 17:20-21, [20] "Now when He was asked by the Pharisees when the kingdom of God would come, He answered them and said, "The kingdom of God does not come with observation; [21]nor will they say, 'See here!' or 'See there!' For indeed, the kingdom of God is within you."

It does not get much clearer than this. This entire drama takes place in heaven, and Jesus himself tells us heaven is within. Therefore Satan, the dragon, and Lucifer are forces within ourselves that set themselves up in opposition to the truth that we are, in reality, the image and likeness of God. That our very life is the presence of God. Just as we each have an individual ego, a virtual self, that keeps us lost in the delusion of detachment and locked within a fragmented universe, we also have this on a collective scale. Carl Jung referred to it as "collective unconscious." When humanity individually and then collectively begins to wake up, through the truth of our Christ identity, and begin to transcend our current privatized splintered selves, the psychic forces that govern this current eon will not go down without a fight.

If a hardcore alcoholic chooses one day to go cold turkey, their entire body will revolt, and they will potentially suffer a seizure. In worst cases, they can die. When we set on the path of Christ consciousness, our old egoic selves will fight to the death to try and hold onto its 'life.' The false self will perceive this as a death of self. In truth, it is only the death of the false self that has kept us opposed to one another and an emergence of our true nature as individualized crystallizations of the presence of the one power, love and life Jehovah will shine forth in its rightful place, and these will be the inhabitants of the Fifth Kingdom. Jesus Christ is the first to achieve this and prepare the way for us to follow. This eventual transcendence into collective Christ consciousness is prophesied in Revelation as the New Jerusalem and the dragon, the devil, will be cast into the lake of fire. "And the devil that deceived them was cast into the lake of fire and brimstone, where the beast and the false prophet are, and shall be tormented day and night forever and ever." In the bible, fire is the symbol of the presence of Jehovah, and water, lake, as we have seen, represents the psyche and mind. So, this passage is telling us that this false self that keeps us in separation, detachment, and fragmentation will no longer hold power over us because we will live in the continual awareness of the omnipresence of Jehovah, I AM.

Let us quickly revisit 2 Peter 1:19, where Peter refers to Christ as the day-star that arises in our hearts. Matter is not evil in itself, it is simply the condensation of spiritual energy and spirit is all good, for God is spirit, and God is good. In its proper relation to spirit, matter is a divine idea as it is through the form of matter that spirit can reflect upon itself (image and likeness of God). In this respect, the matter becomes the light bearer, which is what the name Lucifer means: a container of spirit and is therefore good. Living with the acknowledgment that all life, light, power, wholeness, beauty, joy, and peace come from originating substance we take on the nature of God, which is selfless love and therefore, evil has no place in our minds or hearts because, "perfect love cast out fear,"1 John4:18. Uniting with Jesus Christ, our life becomes hidden in Christ with God (Colossians 3:3) the light of Christ rises, resurrects, within us and this is the emergence of the dawn of day, the day-star (individualization of Jehovah) radiating through us.

THE GARDEN OF GETHSEMANE

Just as the serpent in the Garden of Eden professes that by eating the tree of knowledge of good and evil, our eyes will be opened and cause us to be like God. Jesus is on a tree being crucified between a good thief and a bad or evil thief. Jesus is the way, the truth and the life and so the tree that Jesus is on is the tree of life, which is placed between the tree of good on one side and evil on the other, rectifying the two opposites. As Jesus of Nazareth's spiritual eyes were open and he saw clearly the truth that he is One with God, the very thing that caused us to be cast out of the garden and give birth to the ego, the false self, is now nailed onto the cross in the personage of Jesus the Son of Man and emptied completely of all it's selfish desires by Jesus submission and obedience to the spirit unto its death. This is what Jesus was doing in the Garden of Gethsemane the night before his crucifixion. He asked that the Father take this cup from him if he is willing, but let not "my" will but your will be done. The "my will" is the will of the ego, the personal self. Right after this prayer, it says Jesus was in anguish and sweating drops of blood. If we look at where this takes place, we see he's in the Garden of Gethsemane, which is at the foot of the Mount of olives. Gethsemane in Hebrew means oil press, and so in this garden, olives are squeezed into a pulp, then the pulp is crushed, and the olive oil is produced. Olive oil in ancient times was used to light lamps. What Jesus is doing here is he's paying the price for us to have the right to enter back into the garden of Eden. What cast us out of the Garden was the will of the self, Eve and Adam eating the fruit of the tree for self-satisfaction. This act is being reversed by Jesus taking the personal self that was formed from this act, that part of ourselves that knows we are naked and tries to hide from God. He's submitting it back to God, and this is the pressing out, the drops of blood in his sweat, which becomes an anointed oil for the Holy Spirit to ignite. Meaning our ego, the thing formed to supposedly separate us from God becomes the very thing that allows God to become known to himself within us once it has been completely humbled. That's a lot to understand, so let's break it down further. Something absolutely key to realize here is that we're not entering back into the state Adam and Eve were in before the fall, but we are entering in through Jesus Christ, as in the personal self, called Jesus, being perfectly synthesized with God, the Christ. And this, my friends, is the genius of God! His grand plan from the start. You see, Adam and Eve originally were pure. They had no ego, the personal self came when they ate the fruit for their own selfish pleasure. "Then the eyes of both of them were opened, and they knew that they were naked, and they sewed fig leaves together and made themselves coverings. And they heard the sound of the LORD God walking in the garden in the cool of the day, and Adam and his wife hid themselves from the presence of the LORD God among the trees of the garden. Then the LORD God called to Adam and said to him, "Where are you?" So he said, "I heard Your voice in the garden, and I was afraid because I was naked, and I hid myself." And He said, "Who told you that you were naked? Have you eaten from the tree of which I commanded you that you should not eat?" Genesis 3: 7-

11. Did you catch it? This is what I'm always going on about by saying the personal self. Omniscient God asks, "Where are you?" and "Who told you you were naked?" You see, God is entirely Holy. This means he only ever knows all that is good for the whole at all times, which is complete selflessness. He cannot know selfishness or understand a perspective that is under the delusion that it is separate from him, as there is nothing other than Him. As Isaiah says in chapter 59:2, "But your iniquities have made a separation between you and your God, and your sins have hidden his face from you so that he does not hear." He is all consuming, absolute. And so, in that moment Adam and Eve created within themselves the matrix of a private self that believes it lives entirely independently from the One source of all life, God. This is the origin of Satan, a force that sets itself up in opposition to God by setting up limiting parameters, and believing that sense consciousness, the material universe, has power in and of itself, but the only power evil has is in the perversion and inversion of the one life of God. While we are in this fallen state of consciousness, God cannot know us, and so we cannot know God. This is what Paul is talking about when he says..." But now after you have known God, or rather are known by God", Galatians 4:9. This is a severe statement because, just like Isiah, it's telling us that God does not know us while we are "dead in our sins," because he is the God of the living. "And you He made alive, who were dead in trespasses and sins, in which you once walked according to the course of this world." And so here we are, Jesus, the man, the personal self, going back into the garden and submitting his the personal will to the Holy will of God, pressing out all resistance that the ego puts up to try and hold onto its "life." The produce of this is anointed oil, which is the substance the Holy Spirit uses to illuminate us into conscious union with God, not unconscious servitude as was the case with Adam and Eve. And this brings God's plan to completion. At this moment, the man Jesus

was fully merged into Christ, and there was no longer any distinction between the two. And so, the next day, when Jesus is tortured, mocked, spat on and crucified, it is fully God. himself doing it, not some separate personality, but the one and only God of Gods through the purified ego is known as Jesus of Nazareth. And because God is All in All, being fully self-realized in Jesus, Jesus being a completely pure and righteous conduit for God being, in a way, God is "plugging in" to the flesh of all humanity, causing us all to partake of the crucifixion with Jesus once we have consumed his flesh and blood by partaking in the Holy Communion through faith. By consuming his body in Holy Communion, we are joining ourselves to Jesus' body on the cross, and because that's the moment when all the power that the flesh holds over us, being satans power was killed once and for all, we are now freed from any power and restraints our fleshly mind, our sense consciousness, may have held over us. Satan no longer has any power. The only power he would ever have is the power we allow him to have over us. But in the reality of Christ, he is, and always has been, nothing.

So Must The Son Of Man Be Lifted Up

Just as animal sacrifice played a role in visually releasing humanity from the mental strongholds that kept them bound to suffering, Jesus made the ultimate sacrifice in a dark and powerful ritual. He took it upon himself to liberate humanity from this seemingly impenetrable and opaque mechanical system by offering his body as a gateway to bridge the gap between the temporal and subtle realms. This is what he says in conversation with Nicodemous in John 3 verses 12 through 21:

"If I have told you earthly things and you do not believe, how can you believe if I tell you heavenly things? No one has ascended into heaven except he, who descended from heaven, the Son of Man.

And just as Moses lifted up the serpent in the wilderness as a symbol of salvation, so must the Son of Man be lifted up for all to see, opening the way for whoever believes in him to attain eternal life.

"For God so loved the world, that he gave his only Son, that whoever believes in him should not perish but have eternal life. For God did not send his Son into the world to condemn the world, but in order for the world to be saved through him. Whoever believes in him is not condemned, but whoever does not believe is already condemned because they have not believed in the name of the only Son of God.

And this is the judgment: The light has come into the world, but people loved darkness instead of light because their deeds were evil. Everyone who does wicked things hates the light and avoids it for fear of being exposed. But whoever lives by the truth comes into the light, so that it may be seen plainly that what they have done has been done in God."

By raising up high the crowning effigy of this three-dimensional plane -the human body- for all to look upon and see the very thing that keeps us chained to a cold, remote, segregated reality, Jesus broke and destroyed it once and for all. Only then did he raise it back up, this very same image, to demonstrate that the merging of this dimension with higher dimensions -the kingdom of the heavens- is a reality accessible to all in the here and now. "The kingdom of heaven is at hand," "the kingdom of heaven is within you," "for nothing is secret that shall not be made manifest; neither anything hid that shall not be known and come to light." (Mathew 4:17, Luke 17:21, Luke 8:17).

This line of thinking may help explain the emergence of Gnostic Christianity, with its belief in the ultimate being, the demiurges and his twin brother Lucifer, and humanity being trapped in a fallen universe created by a flawed being under the influence of cosmic Archons. At its heart, this belief portrays mankind as trapped within a corrupt physical and psychological existence that must be broken out of.

As explained in earlier chapters, this is an erroneous line of thought. The integral relationship between Elohim, Jehovah/Christ, humanity, and the true nature of Luciferic or Satanic thought is often misunderstood. It is not that the material plane is inherently corrupt or wrong. In fact, a wise child would not rebel against their parents, who represent limitations to them. Instead, they would understand that the parent's role and the limits of their present circumstances are vital for growth and development into a mature and independent adult.

Similarly, our current three-dimensional reality serves as a training ground for understanding the secrets of higher dimensions in a gradual and natural way. As it states in Romans 1:20, "For since the creation of the world God's invisible qualities - his eternal power and divine nature - have been clearly seen, being understood from what has been made, so that people are without excuse."

As Christians, or those striving to be Christ-like, we are not on this earth simply to thank Jesus for his sacrifice and then wait for our time to float off guilt-free into the afterlife. Our role as the body of Christ and offspring of the I AM is to perpetually manifest the kingdom of heaven - its principles, laws, and knowledge - here on earth in the present moment. We do this by raising our consciousness through meditation on divine principles and embodying the teachings of Jesus Christ.

In John 14:21, Jesus says, "Whoever has my commands and keeps them is the one who loves me. The one who loves me will be loved by my Father, and I too will love them and show myself to them." He was both the first and last to live and communicate this downward causation way of living while still functioning on this earthly level. Through his example, he showed us how to raise our own consciousness to become individualized manifestations of the ONE God.

This is what it truly means to be made in the image and likeness of God. As Christians, it is our duty to continuously strive towards this goal and help raise the consciousness of humanity as a whole.

Jesus Is Jehovah

A lot of Christians believe that Jesus was God but simply a son of God, so not really God, and the actual God is some guy in the sky who loved to punish and kill his son for our evils. We need to realize that Jesus is Jehovah. Therefore, when Jesus is on the cross, it is not some separate entity on the cross dying, it is Jehovah himself on the cross dying. Jesus is Christ, Jehovah is the I Am, and Jesus Christ the Messiah is the visible embodiment of this I Am, as he said to himself, "Most assuredly, I say to you, before Abraham was, I AM." This sentence does not grammatically make sense unless we see that Jesus is saying that he is the omnipresent I AM of Jehovah, which is ancient and infinite and therefore existed before Abraham was born. John puts it as "in the beginning was the word and the word was with God and the word was God" (John1:1). In John 10:34-38 he says, "Jesus answered them, is it not written in your law, I said, Ye are gods? If he called them gods, unto whom the word of God came, and the scripture cannot be broken; Say ye of him, whom the Father hath sanctified, and sent into the world, Thou blasphemest; because I said, I am the Son of God?" Jesus is saying that what he is declaring of himself is nothing new, but in Psalm 82:6, it is written,

"I have said, Ye are gods, and all of you are children of the Most High." Jesus is simply standing up and laying claim to this truth, which had been kept hidden and, over time, forgotten by pharisaical rulers, keepers of the ancient knowledge at that time. Through the material religious bound mentality, this sounds like complete blasphemy, but to those who have awakened to the fact that "we live, move and have our being within God" (Acts 17:28), it is a simple truth, the understanding of which begins the regeneration process of our souls and allows us to begin growing into God. "Assuredly I say to you, that in the regeneration, when the Son of Man sits on the throne of His glory, you who have followed Me will also sit on twelve thrones, judging the twelve tribes of Israel." (Matthew 19:28).

What And Where Is The Kingdom Of Heaven?

From the indistinct time of our pre-conscious state in Eden to our expulsion and, with it, our detached, self-consumed, fragmented state, humanity devolved into a species of war, ruthlessness, self-glorifying and self-gratifying perversion. Kingdoms of supposed enlightenment came but always crumbled as their wisdom was that of mortals, and no real inner spiritual progression was being made.

Kingdoms and civilizations whose power must be protected by earthly weapons are kingdom or civilizations whose power is derived from earthly things and therefore doomed to perish, as all things of the earth perish. A new kind of kingdom then must be established on earth, a kingdom not built or protected with earthly material and earthly weapons, but one that is eternal and can't be touched, violated or attacked by earthly means.

In this kingdom, humanity of all ages will have the ability to evolve within it. To grow and expand, to pass on from generation to generation, that will never deteriorate or crumble but only grow greater and stronger as time progresses.

This kingdom needed a king, but not a king of this earth, as any king of this earth would be doomed to establish a kingdom of this earth and, therefore, would fail as all other kings had failed.

This king would need to establish his kingdom in the hearts, minds, and souls of humanity where it could live and expand, a place where moth and rust cannot destroy or thieves break in a steal. As a seed planted in the soil gradually grows out of the darkness of the earth and reaches toward the heavens, so must this kingdom be established.

This king would establish his kingdom not through force, for force is the language of those still trapped within the separate self, but would establish his kingdom through love, the one and only unifying substance in all creation. He would plant the seeds of his kingdom through speaking the powerful, eternal truths of Jehovah God that would resonate and attach themselves to the core of all who heard, stirring, reawakening within them a deep and ancient memory of a knowledge they feel they once knew but forgot.

This king would have to be born of flesh and walk as humanity walked in order for humanity to be able to follow in his footsteps and clearly be able to distinguish the way forward out of the kingdoms and restraints of this world and into this eternal kingdom. This king is Jesus Christ.

And the kingdom of heaven he taught was not someplace you go to when you die in a galaxy far, far away, but he taught that this kingdom was here and now a present reality within us. He taught that it's a state of conscious harmony and union with God. This is why he always taught about the kingdom of heaven with parables, saying the kingdom of heaven is like so and so because it's not a fixed place but an eternally growing and expanding state of being, of which we are the building blocks.

In many parables, Jesus likened the kingdom of heaven to a seed because a seed has unexpressed capacity. God is infinite potentiality, living spiritual energy comprised of an infinitude of ideas. We are specifically built to be a conscious conduit for these forces, and we tap into and become a current for them through our minds, words and actions.

Once we become impregnated with the various life forces of God's Divine ideals, the next step is to adjust our outer life in accordance with their nature by expressing them to the outer world. For instance, every time we help someone who's down and out by bringing them food, clothes, shelter, giving someone a second chance, choosing forgiveness and selfless love over hatred and bitterness, or helping a single parent family get all the supplies they need to bring some stability to their lives, and so on and so forth, we are bringing the kingdom of heaven into manifestation on the physical plane. We're taking in the Divine ideas of selfless love, compassion, peace, power, strength, and goodwill, dwelling on them until they take root and naturally expand into our outer life.

But unfortunately, the ego of humanity is selfish and lazy and wants everything done for it. And so, when Jesus the promised Messiah came teaching this, it wasn't understood and so not well received. People want a messiah to come and forcefully fix everyone and everything, but fortunately, God doesn't work that way. He's much more subtle, gentle, patient and caring.

Many times, Jesus tried to explain plainly to people what the kingdom of heaven was in the following passages. "My kingdom is not of this world. If my kingdom were of this world, my servants would have been fighting, that I might not be delivered over to the Jews. But my kingdom is not from the world" (John 18:36).

"The kingdom of God is not coming with signs to be observed, nor will they say, 'Look, here it is!' or 'There!' for behold, the kingdom of God is within you" (Luke 17:20).

"The kingdom of God is not eating and drinking (meaning

physical, sensual things) but righteousness and peace and joy in the Holy Spirit."

So, if the kingdom of heaven is within us and it's not a place off somewhere in the clouds that we get beamed to when we die but can actually access it right here right now, then why haven't more people done so?

John The Baptist – Our First Level Of Understanding

John the Baptist was a peculiar and mysterious figure. He stood out amongst the crowds with his unkempt appearance, donned in rough camel skin and subsisting on a diet of locusts and honey. As the cousin of Jesus, his role was to prepare the way for Christ by urging people to cleanse themselves and prepare for the coming of the Kingdom of Heaven.

Living in the wilderness, John embodied a rugged and ascetic lifestyle, representing a period of spiritual growth where truth is often taken in a literal sense. This can lead to self-deprivation and fasting as a means of punishing the flesh, driven by feelings of unworthiness. Just as John lived in a harsh and unforgiving environment, we too may find ourselves struggling to enter into the heavenly kingdom through our own efforts.

The Gospel of Luke reveals that John was born before Jesus, which holds significance when examining biblical themes throughout history. In many stories, there are two states of being described: one earthly and one spiritual. This is evident in the births of Cain before Abel, Ishmael before Isaac, Esau before Jacob, and finally John before Jesus. Each firstborn represents the unregenerated side of humanity, tied to earthly desires and struggles. Cain was a farmer who became a murderer, Ishmael was born to a slave woman and forced into a life in the wilderness, Esau was described as a wild man living off the land with extreme hairiness and hunting skills, and John himself was known as a wild man living in isolation and wearing clothes made from rough camel hair.

These examples make it clear that we are first born into our natural selves but have the opportunity to grow into our spiritual bodies. As Apostle Paul stated, "It is sown a natural body; it is raised a spiritual body." The first man is tied to the earth, while the second man originates from heaven. The journey from our natural state to our spiritual state is not immediate; rather, it is a process of growth and transformation.

John the Baptist is the natural man; he had a high level of understanding, but his understanding was still earthly. Jesus himself said this about John, "Truly I say to you, among those born of women there has not arisen anyone greater than John the Baptist! Yet the one who is least in the kingdom of heaven is greater than he." We see here that there is a structural hierarchy of understanding. John knew the kingdom of heaven was imminent,, but he didn't have the spiritual eyes to see what exactly it was because he had not developed his spiritual body, because he was born before Christ, and so he didn't know the teaching of Christ.

John himself said this about himself, "He (Christ) must increase, but I must decrease. He who comes from above is, above all. He who is of the earth is from the earth and speaks of the earth. He who comes from heaven is above all."

John the Baptist was the herald of the coming Messiah, Jesus. A voice crying in the wilderness, repent, which has its root meaning in the word metanoia, which means a complete and radical inner transformation of self.

Before we can consciously evolve from our earthly understanding to a spiritualized understanding, we must first cleanse our minds from the way we perceived the world before. When Jesus is talking about John the Baptist, he says, "And no man puts a bit of new cloth on an old coat, for by pulling away from the old, it makes a worse hole." Clothes in the bible represent our psychological makeup, and Jesus is telling us that you can't take a new teaching and try to weave it into your previous limited opinions and perceptions. Otherwise there will inevitably come along an inner conflict. In order to truly take in new teaching, you have to cleanse your mind of everything you knew before and allow the new to take root.

But as humans, we can't just change ourselves immediately. In order for a transmutation of consciousness to take place, we need to establish a network of ideas that will gradually lift us to a state of consciousness that transcends the current one. This network of ideas through which transformation takes place is the ideal of the Kingdom of Heaven.

The Kingdom of Heaven stands above and beyond all material limitation and restriction and keeps humanity evolving, ascending to infinitely higher and higher states of consciousness, or another way to put it would be subtler depths of meaning, as it is the Kingdom, ordered realm, of divine ideals. "Repent (metanoia) for the kingdom of heaven is at hand!" or radically change your state of consciousness to see and know that the kingdom of heaven is here and now, as John the Baptist preached in the wilderness.

Water in the bible is the symbol of the psyche and mental potentiality, which clearly fits John's message of metanoia, cleansing, completely renewing the mind and turning it toward spiritual truth. In order for us to receive Christ, we must each first go through this process of metanoia, psychological baptism. A complete denial of all earthly pride, attachment and ego driven desires, "If anyone desires to come after Me, let him deny himself, and take up his cross, and follow Me"(Matthew 16:24). This psychological baptism turns our consciousness away from the elemental, sensory world, and toward the subtle essences of spiritual truth and meaning.

A strange statement Jesus makes about John and the kingdom is this, "From the days of John the Baptist until now, the kingdom of heaven has suffered violence, and forceful people lay hold of it." How can you violently lay hold of the kingdom of heaven? John, and his followers approached idea of the kingdom of heaven from the outside in. John taught the scriptures from an earthly understanding, and so they thought that by fasting, dressing in uncomfortable clothing, punishing the flesh, living in the harsh environment of the wilderness and keeping the Mosaic law flawlessly, they would be worthy of the kingdom.

We can't break into the kingdom of heaven. All we can do is humble and sanctify ourselves, not by punishing and starving the flesh, but through a psychological sanctification of releasing, denying and detaching ourselves from all of our previous limited beliefs, addictions and selfish love. By doing this, we till the soil of our hearts and make it ready for the Truth to be planted. John could only understand this from a psychological perspective, but not from a spiritual one, and so prepared the way for the spiritual man, Jesus, the best he knew how.

As he said, "I indeed baptize you with water unto repentance (metanoia), but He who is coming after me is mightier than I, whose sandals I am not worthy to carry. He will baptize you with the Holy Spirit and fire"(Matthew 3:11).

John represents the intellectual perception of Truth within all of us. That part of us that reaches a point where we're ready to turn away from the world and stop looking for answers in it because we know it's just a wilderness that has no life in itself. All we can do is soak our minds with the word of God by reading scripture and waiting for Christ to meet us where we're at so that the Holy Spirit may descend upon us and raise us to union with God.

The John in us is like the first stage of the sleeper waking up. Something stirs us awake, and at first, we start becoming conscious of faint sounds around us. Then our eyes open a little, and we see the world through blurry eyes and a groggy head. But slowly, we'll start waking up more and more until the dawn of the light of Christ awakens us fully into the perception of a new reality. The only reality is our individuality in God through Christ. As the Apostle Paul says, "But all things become visible when they are exposed by the light, for everything that becomes visible is light. For this reason, it says.

The Language Of Parables

As the chapter on John the Baptist revealed, every person is comprised of two distinct sides - the outer and inner. The outer side is the one we are born into, ruled by our false-self or personality. It is through this side that we interact with and navigate through the systems of the world. We spend our lives building and working on this side, shaping it through our experiences in the outer world. It is a private and personal self, one that we believe we have complete ownership over.

But there is also an inner side, undeveloped and lying dormant within each of us. This side is innate, something we are all born with and cannot escape from. It is the spark of life, our I Am-ness, freely given to us all. However, it often becomes smothered and suffocated by our pridefully built ego, our personality.

In this material universe, our purpose is to develop this inner side. Yet, it cannot be forced or achieved through following laws or guidelines. Rather, it must be done on an individual level through our own inner understanding. Instead of building up as our personality desires, the growth of this inner side comes from stripping away everything that the personality clings onto as its own.

However, the personality is a matrix, a vast network that acts like a web that catches and eats anything that falls into it that isn't part of the system it's established.

It acts as a fortress, constantly on guard to catch and consume anything that does not align with its established system. Therefore, the Truth of one's inner life cannot simply be accepted at face value; it must penetrate through the layers of protection and resistance put up by the outer self.

To bypass this false self, Jesus tells stories using familiar earthly concepts such as farming, seeds, trees, fishing, weddings, and more. These stories may seem simple on the surface, but within them lie eternal truths that have the power to transform the isolated darkness within us into an expansive kingdom of light.

There are three distinct layers to all scripture: literal/historical, psychological, and spiritual. Only by meditating on the words can we unlock the deeper spiritual meanings hidden within them. This process allows the Holy Spirit to activate and release the potential contained within each word, opening our spiritual eyes to new levels of understanding.

Another way to view this is to see the universe as an infinite collection of forms, condensed manifestations of information. By perceiving reality through the lens of the Holy Spirit, we begin to see beyond the physical forms and into the essence and meaning behind them. Just as hair grows out of a body or grass grows out of the earth, all forms in this universe grow out of the omnipresent and omniscient Jehovah.

God is meaning, and so by intuitively reading the information each form contains, by understanding its relation to everything around it, the universe begins to unfold, or more accurately in-fold itself, and comes alive to us as meaning.

Our earthly minds, the intellect, can't do this, and so the bible remains a sealed book to those who haven't received the Holy Spirit, and therefore, sounds completely contradictory and stupid to them. But as with everything in life, the unfoldment of spiritual understanding is a gradual process, and we, therefore, must first comprehend the literal meaning, the form, which gives way to the psychological, which finally gives way to the spiritual.

The Hebrew sages wrote the bible in the language of roots and branches. The eternal divine qualities of Jehovah can't be put into words, and they can only be experienced. However, we can tune our minds to their reality by thinking about and meditating on Truth. Because consciousness is life, whatever we keep our awareness on for an extended period of time opens itself up to us. Just like rose petals gradually open up to the sun. Exactly like analyzing a tree, by looking at how the branches spread out and expand from a single source, the trunk, we can know that the unseen part of the tree is of the same nature.

The language of parables can be compared to a user interface on a computer, where we may not understand the coding behind it but can easily navigate through it using Windows. Similarly, the parables serve as an interface between our earthly understanding and the hidden, deeper meanings of Truth. Just as Jesus spoke in parables to reveal the mysteries of the kingdom of heaven, we, too, can access these hidden truths by immersing ourselves in meditation and visualization of these stories. Through this process, the seed of Truth takes root within us and propels our evolution towards spiritual enlightenment. Let us remember the words of Matthew 13:34, "All these things Jesus spoke to the crowds in parables, and He did not speak to them without a parable. This is to fulfill what was spoken through the prophet: 'I will open my mouth in parables; I will utter things hidden since the foundation of the world.'" So let us embrace the parables as technological tools for our spiritual growth and awaken to the realization that the kingdom of heaven already resides within each of us, waiting to be discovered through our alignment with divine Truth.

The Parable Of The Sower

The parable of the Sower goes like this...and it goes like this. "A farmer went out to sow his seed. 4 As he was scattering the seed, some fell along the path, and the birds came and ate it up. 5 Some fell on rocky places where it did not much soil. It sprang up quickly because the soil was shallow. 6 But when the sun came up, the plants were scorched, and they withered because they had no root. 7 Other seeds fell among thorns, which grew up and choked the plants. 8 Still other seed fell on good soil, where it produced a crop - a hundred, sixty or thirty times what was sown. 9 Whoever has ears, let them hear."

He then gives his explanation to the disciples, as this first parable, Jesus tells us is the parable of parables and the starting point for all to understand what the true kingdom of heaven is. "When anyone hears the message about the kingdom and does not understand it, the evil one comes and snatches away what was sown in their heart. This is the seed sown along the path. 20 The seed falling on rocky ground refers to someone who hears the word and at once receives it with joy. 21 But since they have no roots, they last only a short time. When trouble or persecution comes because of the word, they quickly fall away. 22 The seed falling among the thorns refers to someone who hears the word, but the worries of this life and the deceitfulness of wealth choke the word, making it unfruitful. 23 But the seed falling on good soil refers to someone who hears the word and understands it. This is the one who produces a crop, yielding a hundred, sixty or thirty times what was sown."

We were once only aware of goodness, but now we also have knowledge of evil. This shift within ourselves was a realization that a part of us was no longer united with God.

Under the illusion of being separate individuals, we then left the garden or what was perceived as the presence of God. This marked the beginning of time and space. However, God is all-knowing, omnipresent, and eternal, so there is nowhere to hide from His presence. For our own sake, God created a veil over our consciousness - an illusion of a private self where we can move through time and space, think, feel, experience, and catalog memories, believing that we are progressing towards something.

But this is not God's ultimate plan for us. His plan is for each of us to reach a point where we become compatible with Him once again - where we can exist in the truth of His omnipresence and omniscience without feeling condemned. This is where Jesus comes in. He is the fully realized God-man who burned away the veil of the private self and fearlessly expressed himself as the individualization of God Almighty! He did this so that we would follow in his footsteps; he paid the price that humanity needed to witness in order for us to undergo such a radical inner transformation.

He is the final step in human evolution - the firstborn of creation who is no longer just a creature but a creator. So, to summarize: humanity went from being unconsciously united with God in the garden to consciously perceiving isolation and finally reaching full conscious and willing union with God, becoming His image and likeness with complete freedom in Him. And this is the very purpose of our three-dimensional universe - to grow our soul body in reunion with God.

This potential within us can be awakened and nurtured by fertilizing it with Truth, light, and life from Christ. By "putting on Christ" and elevating our earthly and sensory consciousness to the level of eternal spiritual principle. As Jesus said, "And when I am lifted up from the earth, I will draw everyone to myself."

Let us now delve back into the parable of the Sower, told by Christ himself. Picture a humble man carrying a worn bag of seeds, walking through a vast field of rich and fertile soil, bathed in perfect sunlight. With careful hands, he scatters the tiny seeds all around him, trusting that they will grow and flourish in this ideal environment. And indeed, as time passes, these little seeds sprout and blossom into a bountiful harvest - 30 times greater than what was originally sown. The man rejoices and collects the precious seeds from the fruit, returning them to his bag, which now contains a wealth of blessings. This is the lesson that Christ imparts to us: our purpose in life is to nurture and cultivate our souls, just like a farmer cares for his crops. We must take the seed of Truth planted within us and allow it to take root through understanding and contemplation. As it grows and flourishes, it unlocks our true potential and awakens divine attributes within our souls. This continuous process leads to a deeper connection with God and a greater understanding of His love and teachings. Through internalizing the story of Christ's crucifixion and resurrection, we embark on a journey towards spiritual awakening where our egos and personal desires fade away, leaving us standing in the kingdom of heaven on earth. And there, we join in chorus with the angels, proclaiming, "Holy, Holy, Holy is the Lord of hosts; the whole earth is full of his glory." (Isaiah 6:3).

Parable Of The Wheat And The Tares

The second parable Christ gives to help us understand the nature of the kingdom of heaven is the parable of the wheat and tares, and it goes like this. "24 Here is another story Jesus told: "The Kingdom of Heaven is like a farmer who planted good seed in his field. 25 But that night, as the workers slept, his enemy came and planted weeds among the wheat, then slipped away. 26 When the crop began to grow and produce grain, the weeds also grew.

27 "The farmer's workers went to him and said, 'Sir, the field where you planted that good seed is full of weeds! Where did they come from?' 28 "'An enemy has done this!' the farmer exclaimed. "'Should we pull out the weeds?' they asked.

29 "'No,' he replied, 'you'll uproot the wheat if you do. 30 Let both grow together until the harvest. Then I will tell the harvesters to sort out the weeds, tie them into bundles, and burn them, and to put the wheat in the barn.'"

In Jesus' explanation of this parable to his disciples, he explains that The Son of Man is the Sower. As Jesus says in Matthew 13:17, " I tell you the truth, many prophets and righteous people longed to see what you see, but they didn't see it. And they longed to hear what you hear, but they didn't hear it." He's telling us that he's the Son of Man who is sowing this truth about the kingdom into the hearts of humanity. He explains that the field in the parable is the world. The world that we experience is an aggregation of all people's thoughts, ideas and beliefs.

The internet can be seen as a reflection of the current psychological and spiritual state of humanity. It serves as a mirror, constantly reflecting what is in our hearts. Jesus explains that the good seed represents the people of the kingdom - those who are conduits for Christ's wisdom and life, bearing good fruit throughout all seasons. As we transform ourselves by renewing our minds with God's eternal principles, we bring forth these truths into manifestation and ultimately create heaven on earth.

However, Jesus also warns us that weeds can be sown among the good seed while workers sleep. This refers to a psychological slumber, as urged repeatedly in scripture to stay alert. We must be consciously present in each moment and take every thought captive to follow Christ's teachings. When we allow worldly concerns such as money, work, or temptations to cloud our minds, our consciousness becomes restricted and trapped by the limitations of our senses. This is akin to being asleep, allowing the material world to control our psychological well-being instead of staying connected to God's boundless love. In this state, we are imprisoned by the false self, also known as Satan the accuser, who sows weeds in our perception while we are consumed by the troubles of this three-dimensional realm.

The workers think that they should immediately pull the weeds up, but the, farmer knows that doing so will also uproot the wheat and tells them to leave it until the wheat is mature and ready to harvest. Then, the reapers will pull the tares and burn them but take the wheat into the barn. During the development of our spiritual body and our soul, we're eating the tree of life, which is the wisdom and truth of Christ, which is a gradual process of growing into that which is good, constructive and life-giving. But we cannot expect to be a mature Christian right away and so while we lapse and fall back into our false-self state of being, senses consciousness, hurtful, error thoughts are sown also.

The thing is, though, that consciousness is life, and it grows whatever it focuses on. Jesus knows this and so instructs us not to put too much of our attention on the negative, evil things, as that will cause them to amplify, and we are not spiritually strong enough at this stage to do this without snuffing out the light of good, which is the truth, within us also. It is the same meaning as when he tells us to "resist not evil, but whoever slaps you on the right cheek, turn the other to him also." By resisting something, we strengthen it with the life of our consciousness.

And so, he instructs us to wait until both the weeds and the wheat are fully grown and ready to harvest, at which time, he says, the reapers come and take the weeds to burn them, and the wheat is collected into the barn. In his explanation he says that the angels are the ones who do the reaping. When Yahweh communicates with us, the filter of our mind crystalizes the intention of God's ideal into a definite concept or action. This concept or action is wholistic and pure, direct from God, and therefore perceived as an angel, as angels are messengers, guides and protectors, which, in this case, will come and destroy any lingering darkness within us.

There will come a time where, if we have persisted in keeping our attention focused on the good only and have spiritually matured enough to see that the desires and lusts of this world will never bring lasting satisfaction but only enslavement to a lower level of reality, then we reach a point where we want God to burn up all things that are not of Him in the fire of his Holy presence. In John 14:21, Jesus says, "Those who accept my commandments and obey them are the ones who love me. And because they love me, my

Father will love them. And I will love them and reveal, myself, to each of them." In Jesus' explanation of this parable, he says that the weeds are burned up in a furnace of fire, but the righteous will shine forth like the sun in the kingdom of our Father. It is the same fire that burns up all negative attachment and enslavement to this 3-dimensional world, but then those who are in alignment with God's principles, instead of burning by this fire, amplify and radiate it like the sun. The sun brings life, warmth and knowledge to all around, and so it is with the sons and daughters of the kingdom.

So, we see that by staying in alignment with God's eternal principles of peace, love, harmony, joy, etc., within us, and extending that to everyone around us, even our supposed enemies, we grow into God enough to where Christ himself will be revealed to us. When this happens, we will reap the good that the destruction of sense consciousness brings and experience the power and illumination that comes from our spiritual re-birth, transformation and maturity.

THE PARABLE OF THE MUSTARD SEED AND THE LEAVEN

I'm going to combine these two parables as they're both short and related to each other. First is the parable of the mustard seed. It goes like this...

"The kingdom of heaven is like a mustard seed, which a man took and sowed in his field, 32 which indeed is the least of all the seeds; but when it is grown, it is greater than the herbs and becomes a tree, so that the birds of the air come and nest in its branches."

The next is the Leaven. "Another parable He spoke to them: "The kingdom of heaven is like leaven, which a woman took and hid in three measures of meal till it was all leavened."

Let's break down the main points here. The man and woman both take the seed and leaven, and they do something with it. They use their hands to take these items. Throughout history, the hand has been seen as a symbol of power. With our hands, we can take what we want, exert our authority, or create things.

The first parable of the Sower describes how we, humanity, are the material in which the teaching of the kingdom is sown. The second is the parable of how good and evil grow within us until a time when we choose the good and discard the evil. Now comes the next stage, which is how we're to take hold of this teaching and what we're to do with it.

When we take something, we choose a definite action: the man with the mustard seed takes the seed and then sows it in his field. His field means within himself, as we have our internal state, which is our own, and an external world which we don't own. From here grows the tree. Starting from the lower material level of earth, the ground, into the sky, which represents the kingdom of heaven, Not because we actually think there's a literal kingdom in the sky, but spiritually discerned the earth is dense, hard, limiting, opaque, and the sky is open, limitless, clear, and a place from which we can get a holistic vision of the earth, and so analogues with the heavenly realms.

Birds of the air come and rest in its branches meaning higher, subtler, fuller, levels of meaning come to the Sower, that are far above the sense-based consciousness of earth. Whereas our level of spiritual understanding begins in the darkness of the earth, the roots of truth build the stable foundation from which the trunk, branches and leaves can grow and expand into finer and finer levels of meaning that were once inaccessible for us to understand. "First in the natural, then in the spiritual."

Let's look at the second parable of the woman. Instead of man. Seed. And ground. We have women. Leaven. Meal. The man took his seed and sowed it into the ground. This woman also takes it, but instead, she hides it in 3 measures of meal. Why does she hide it? In Matthew 16:6, Jesus says, "Take heed and beware of the leaven of the Pharisees and the Sadducees." 7 And they (the disciples) reasoned among themselves, saying, "It is because we have taken no bread."

It's pretty comical that even his disciples took him literally here and thought he was talking about actual bread. But if we continue, Jesus goes on to say, "11 How is it you do not understand that I did not speak to you concerning bread? But to beware of the leaven of the Pharisees and Sadducees." 12 Then they understood that He did not tell them to beware of the leaven of bread but of the doctrine of the Pharisees and Sadducees.

Throughout Jesus's ministry, he was merciless toward the way the Pharisees and Sadducees acted and conducted their religious beliefs. Why? Because they did everything for the approval of men.

They wanted to appear holy, act holy, and be admired for their spiritual stature and titles by other people. Their entire way of being was externally focused, purposefully out in the open for all to see. Now, what did the woman of the parable do, though? She took Jesus' teaching, and she hid it within herself. Slowly, quietly, in privacy, without needing confirmation or adoration from anyone, the leaven, Jesus' teaching grew within her.

It says she hid it within 3 measures of meal. The number 3 represents completion because the duality, or seeming separation, of 1 and 2 unite, and three is the embodiment of their unification. So, three measures of meal can be seen as the full absorption of the teaching into her mind, body and soul.

So, to recap, first, we have the man who takes the seed, plants it in his field, meaning within himself, and slowly but surely, this small seed, which is the smallest of all, unassuming to those who don't see its value, grows deep from within, out into every branch of our life, where eventually higher ideas from divine mind come and make their home within it. This is a mental approach to growing within the kingdom of heaven. Our consciousness is becoming more and more attuned to finer and finer layers of meaning.

The second method of growing within the kingdom of heaven is to take the good of Jesus' teaching, hide it within our hearts and overtime, it grows and expands until the divine revelation of its reality takes over our entire being.

In the next two parables, Jesus teaches us about the kingdom of heaven and instructs us about what we must be willing to personally sacrifice to commit ourselves fully to the process of inner evolution into the kingdom.

The Hidden Treasure and the Pearl of Great Price

Jesus tells two more short parables to describe to us what the kingdom of heaven is like. The first one is the hidden treasure.

"Again, the kingdom of heaven is like treasure hidden in a field, which a man found and hid; and for joy over it, he goes and sells all that he has and buys that field." Again, the kingdom of heaven is like a merchant seeking beautiful pearls, who, when he had found one pearl of great price, went and sold all that he had and bought it."

These parables are based on what we individually, internally, must do in order to reach the evolutionary stage called the kingdom of heaven. We must know what is worthy of buying and what is worthy of selling in exchange for it, or be a good merchant, and use our reasoning powers to barter with our personal self and work out our own salvation.

There isn't a much better symbol for the soul than a pearl. Pearls are created by a foreign substance entering the oyster's shell, and over time, to protect itself from this irritant, the oyster builds up layers of mucus to cover it, and eventually, the pearl is formed. This is the perfect analogy for how our soul body is built here on this earth. Through this physical experience, temptations and trials always come (the foreign particles), but over time, we can learn to not give in to selfish passions and lustful desires, as they're irritants that don't bring lasting joy. So, we learn to submit them to God in humility and selflessness. Once we do this, we experience the soothing presence of the holy spirit, coating our hearts, so we no longer burn with lustful passions, but instead, our spiritual body is built up, and the dross burned away, in the refining fires of God. In Revelation 21:21, we see that the gates to the New Jerusalem, or as Paul calls it, the Heavenly Jerusalem, are made of pearl. Just as a gate is a transitional point for leaving one place and entering another, our soul, now matured in Christ, stands as the border that bridges the gap between our physical body and the unveiled presence of God, which is the kingdom of heaven. This happens to us when, just like Peter, representing faith, the spirit reveals to us that Jesus is Christ. With that revelation, we are given the keys to the kingdom, which locks and unlocks the pearl gates, just as Jesus tells Peter after he realizes Jesus is Christ, "I will give you the keys of the kingdom of heaven; whatever you bind on earth will be bound in heaven, and whatever you loose on earth will be loosed in heaven."

We start off by trying to find beautiful pearls in our outer life. Food, sex, shelter, money, power, knowledge, but we eventually find no real truth in any of these, and so we hopefully reach a point where we know what we need can't come from this earth. And so, we're ready to sell them all for the one pearl that comes at a great price.

In Matthew 19:21-22 a rich young prince comes to Jesus and asks how he can have eternal life. Jesus responds, "If you want to be perfect, go, sell what you have and give to the poor, and you will have treasure in heaven; and come, follow Me." But when the young man heard that saying, he went away sorrowful, for he had great possessions."

Jesus was testing the prince to see where his heart lay. If the young prince gladly told Jesus yes, Lord, and was about to go sell all he had, Jesus would have stopped him and said you have the kingdom already. Just as in Luke 34, he says, "Where your treasure is there, your heart will be also." If we sow our desires into things of the flesh and this earth, then we'll be chained to those desires and so unable to internally evolve, as everything on this earth is an effect and doesn't have life within itself, and so can't bring lasting satisfaction.

But, if we sow in the spirit, in line with God's eternal principals, then we'll inherit these things which will last eternally and accompany us in the higher dimensions of heaven. Paul puts it like this in Galatians 6:8, "Those who live only to satisfy their own sinful nature will harvest decay and death from that sinful nature. But those who live to please the Spirit will harvest everlasting life from the Spirit."

And so, we see in both the man who found the hidden treasure and the merchant who found the pearl of great price the willingness to sell off everything they owned because of this one treasure and pearl, which they knew was of infinitely greater value than anything they had previously owned. They needed to discard, clear out, and let go of the old parts of themselves in order to make way for this new treasure.

You can't put old wine into new wine skins, meaning you can't try to change and morph new teaching to fit your old pre-conceived notions, prejudices and limited understanding. You've got to be completely willing to let it all go! Realize that all the material universe is simply an effect, a condensation of divine ideals, and in and of itself, there is no life and, therefore, no fulfillment.

We only begin to truly come alive when we plug ourselves directly into first cause, and the channel through which we do this is through the renewing or transformation of our mind. Once we have become reborn, our soul needs to be fed, and the food our soul feeds on is the word or Truth of God. We must eat our daily bread, or another way to put it is, by taking into ourselves and assimilating eternal ideals, our soul body grows, strengthens and matures until we are anchored in inner peace, love, joy, knowledge, wisdom, understanding, power and confidence. The allure and temptation of the physical world begin to become dimmer and dimmer and no longer hold the sway they once used to. It's then that we'll have eyes to see and perceive what the true treasure really is and be willing to give up everything for it.

PARABLE OF THE NET

In the 7th parable, Jesus teaches about the kingdom of heaven, in the gospel of Matthew, is the parable about the net, and it goes like this. "Once again, the kingdom of heaven is like a net that was let down into the lake and caught all kinds of fish. When it was full, the fishermen pulled it up on the shore. Then they sat down and collected the good fish in baskets but threw the bad away. This is how it will be at the end of the age. The angels will come and separate the wicked from the righteous and throw them into the blazing furnace, where there will be weeping and gnashing of teeth.

Firstly, in Matthew's gospel, this is the 7th parable. 7 is the most used number in the bible, and it always indicates some form of completion. As most of us know, God created the heavens and the earth in 7 stages. We each individually must go through 7 stages of inner evolution to reach complete unity with God as is mapped out in the Book of revelation. So, we can see that within these 7 parables of the teaching of the Kingdom of Heaven, Jesus has laid out for us a clear picture of what the kingdom of heaven is, enough for us to get started on the right path at least.

Jesus uses the metaphor of a net cast into a lake. The net represents our mind, which is a matrix collecting and cataloging all kinds of information, thoughts and ideas, both good and bad.

Fish in the bible represent thoughts and ideas. Each thought we have is metaphysically attached to a stream of other thoughts, all of which belong to a great web of an overarching idea.

If we look at John 21: verse 5-6, it says, "He called out to them, "Friends, haven't you any fish?" "No," they answered. He said, "Throw your net on the right side of the boat, and you will find some." When they did, they were unable to haul the net in because of the large number of fish. All the philosophies and psychologies of the world have done nothing to bring true and lasting enlightenment to humanity. And this is because we're all operating within the perceived confines of our limited human nature.

But once we recognize, listen to, and obey Christ-Mind, then we have cast our nets on the right side, and abundance follows. Meaning that where we once operated from the viewpoint of lack and limitation, we now embody the viewpoint of the eternal Christ, within which there is only infinite life and potentiality.

COMMON SYMBOLIC MOTIFS THROUGHOUT THE BIBLE

<u>THE VINEYARD:</u>

The vineyard has long been revered in the bible, its presence intertwined with the imagery of wine, which symbolizes the journey toward spiritual growth. In John 15:5, Jesus proclaims, "I am the vine, and you are the branches," illustrating the importance of our connection to Him for our transformation. Just as wine is made from grapes that have undergone a process of maturation, so must we experience a spiritual evolution through our time in the vineyard.

But why is the vineyard specifically chosen as the setting for this transformation? It can be seen as representative of both nurturing and discipline. Just as vines require diligent care and pruning to produce high-quality grapes, our souls need to undergo a similar process to reach their full potential. Without proper attention, the vines may produce an excess of unripe grapes, just as without proper guidance and discipline, our souls may not fully ripen.

The vineyard, with its rows upon rows of lush green vines and ripe, juicy grapes, carries a symbolic weight reminiscent of the biblical tale of Adam and Eve. Just as the tree of knowledge played a central role in the story of humanity's separation from God, so too does the vineyard represent our earthly journey toward salvation through growth and learning. Our sense of self, often referred to as a "false self," enables us to navigate through life's challenges and mistakes while seeking God's guidance and ultimate redemption. This parallel can also be seen in how God led the Israelites through the wilderness with a guiding cloud and pillar of fire, providing them with protection and direction on their journey toward spiritual fulfillment. The vibrant colors and rich symbolism of the vineyard serve as a reminder of our human journey toward enlightenment and closeness with God.

Throughout the pages of the Bible, Israel is often portrayed as a sprawling vineyard (Hosea 10:1, Psalms 80:8, Isaiah 5:1-7) where life and growth are constantly intertwined. Jesus himself frequently uses parables involving vineyards to convey profound spiritual lessons to his followers. However, even with diligent preparation and careful cultivation, there are times when wild or imperfect fruits are produced - just like how in Isaiah 5:1-7, despite all efforts, only bitter grapes were yielded. This serves as a powerful reminder that our journey toward spiritual maturity is not always a smooth ride; at times, it requires starting over from scratch through the Tree of knowledge method. Through the challenges and lessons learned in the vineyard, we can strive towards developing a strong and fruitful relationship with God as we continue on our paths toward eternal salvation. The vineyard itself is a metaphor for the complexities of faith, with its winding rows of vines and unexpected twists and turns. Yet through perseverance and dedication, good fruit can be produced, and our connection with God can grow deeper and more fulfilling, as long as we always keep Christ as our vine and not the wine of our own sowing.

Let us delve into the curious tale of Noah, who, soon after surviving the great flood, decides to plant a vineyard and ends up in a state of drunkenness and vulnerability (Genesis 9:20-21). While there is much to analyze in these verses, our focus will be on uncovering the true motivation behind Noah's actions. As we have previously discussed, Adam and Eve once shared a complete connection with God - a symbiotic consciousness akin to that of an unborn child where all needs are immediately met without any concept of space, time, or hunger. The potent effects of wine can induce a similar state of being, one that blurs the lines between reality and divine unity. Perhaps this is why Noah turned to it after experiencing such a momentous event as the catastrophic flood. In his intoxicated state, he may have sought solace in the familiarity and comfort of that primal connection with God.

The effects of wine on the mind and body are known to induce a state of altered consciousness. It can strip away inhibitions, instill feelings of confidence and relaxation, and bring about a sense of joy. Noah, in planting his vineyard, attempted to recreate the state of being found in the Garden of Eden. However, unlike Cain, who tilled the soil with sweat and determination, Noah's efforts were focused on cultivating the earth and producing wine. This act was noble and worthy, but it would never be enough to enter into the presence of God solely through personal effort. It is like trying to break into a fortified vault with bare hands.

Yet, we see in Jesus' first miracle at the wedding in Cana that he turns water into wine. The vessels he instructs his servants to fill were six ceremonial stone jars. The number six symbolizes man, as man was created on the sixth day. As the previous video on symbolic meanings has taught us, stone represents a stable foundation upon which to establish truth. These were not just any stone jars, they were ceremonial -; they were ceremonial jars meant for sacred purposes.

When we put all of this together, we see that these six stone jars represent mankind's attempt at understanding and carrying the truth of God. This is good, but it is only at the level of water - our earthly understanding and base literal interpretation of truth represented by the stone jars. We need something more, and we need New Wine - a complete internal transformation that can only come from God himself, not through our own efforts.

As the wedding guests sipped from their glasses and marveled at the rich, velvety taste of the wine, they were unaware of the deeper symbolism behind Jesus' miracle. The transformation of water into wine represented a greater transformation - the journey from human understanding (symbolized by humble jars) to divine wisdom (represented by the finest wine). It was a reminder that true spiritual enlightenment can only come from God and not through our own struggles and efforts. At that moment, as the sweet aroma of the wine-filled their senses, it was a powerful lesson in surrendering to a higher power and allowing ourselves to be transformed into vessels of divine knowledge and understanding.

As Jesus performs his first miracle, the atmosphere is filled with a sense of anticipation and wonder. With a simple touch, he transforms water - the symbol of psychological understanding - into the finest wine, a clear representation of the New and most exquisite truth that he brings to the world. The jars holding this water are made of sturdy stone, reflective of the old ways and traditions that are being left behind in exchange for something new and divine.

This transformation is not achieved through labor, struggle or strife, but rather through the power of Christ's presence within us. Like leaven in his parables, his teachings expand our minds and open us up to metaphysical truths that were previously unknown. No longer dependent on the work of others, we now have a direct connection to God within ourselves. We no longer need to rely on our neighbor's vineyard to sustain us, for Christ is our vine - not from the tree of knowledge of good and evil, but from the tree of life itself.

And as we continue to grow and spread forth like branches from this divine vine, we produce a new kind of wine - one that fills us with bliss and conscious union with God. Through this awareness, we understand that God's goodness is constantly pouring forth through us into the world, like an endless stream of pristine wine. Later, this wine would be his very own blood. This is the free gift of his very self given to us, and it is our duty to share it with others and spread its joy throughout the world.

<u>WINE:</u>

As we delve into the symbolism of wine in the Bible, it's important to note that this method only applies to red wine. The deep, rich color of red symbolizes the blood of Christ and his sacrifice for humanity. In contrast, white wine is made in a different, almost opposite process, with its pale, golden hue representing purity and innocence. Understanding the intricacies of wine-making is crucial if we want a deeper understanding of why it is used in numerous parables, miracles, and symbols throughout both the Old and New Testaments. It is a powerful metaphor for spiritual transformation and growth.

To create wine, grapes are carefully selected and crushed to release their juice. This juice represents our various states of consciousness and the potential for growth within each individual. Yeast, often seen as a representation of the ego or personal self, is then added to the vat. Just as yeast feeds on sugar to produce alcohol, our egos feed on selfish desires and pleasures that can hinder our spiritual growth.

The fermentation process that follows is akin to our own journey toward enlightenment. As the yeast consumes the sugar in the grape juice and produces alcohol, we must also learn to let go of our egos and dissolve them into God's will. This is represented by new wine – pure and free from the taint of selfish desires.

And just as wines age by sitting on their lees (dead yeast and grape skins), so too do we continue to grow and develop as we progress along our spiritual journey. Over time, fragrant chemicals are released from these elements and blend into the liquor, giving wines their distinct flavors. Similarly, as we dissolve our egos and become more aligned with God's will, we begin to radiate a unique essence that reflects our spiritual growth.

The longer a wine sits on its sediments, the more robust and flavorful it becomes. In the same way, those who are ready for their regeneration are plucked during harvest time – a metaphor for the end of our physical lives and the beginning of our spiritual journey.

As we have discussed in other teachings, this three-dimensional universe of time and space exists for us to develop our soul body. Each experience and lesson helps us shed our selfish desires (represented by consuming sugar) and transform into selfless beings who seek to benefit the whole. This process releases fermenting chemicals that add flavor to the alcohol and make it more enjoyable – just as our transformation into loving, compassionate individuals adds depth and richness to our spiritual growth.

The ego, like yeast, is initially focused on satisfying its own desires by consuming the sweetness of life. It hungers for pleasure and gratification, seeking to fill itself with worldly delights. However, as we begin to cultivate a network of truthful ideas in our minds, we can transform these selfish pleasures into something that helps us grow spiritually and kills off the ego. This process is like a delicate dance as we learn to balance the desires of the ego with the wisdom of eternal truths. Slowly but surely, we bring our ego down to its lowest level and teach it to become selfless.

As a result, the once-dominant and ego-driven yeast and grape skins begin to release delightful flavors and play their part in the natural order of life. The resulting alcohol absorbs these fragrant chemicals and matures into a rich and diverse flavor, now joined with a transformative substance - the eternal truths of God or "new wine," as Jesus refers to it. Swirling in the glass, this new wine embodies the essence of growth, transformation, and enlightenment.

It's important to note that we can never completely get rid of our ego; it was created for a purpose. But through the process of our soul's development and focusing on eternal truth, our ego learns to transmute its selfish drives into something that adds more depth and richness to our lives. It becomes like a chisel, carving away at our rough edges and revealing the true beauty within.

Just as wine ages and matures over time, so too are we on our journey towards spiritual maturity. Each experience, each lesson learned, adds another layer of complexity and depth to our being. And just as each bottle of wine represents its own unique blend of grapes and aging processes, each person represents a drop in the collective vat of consciousness and soul development. As we learn from those who have overcome their egos before us, we continue to add wisdom and knowledge until we collectively reach a state of matured and mellow new wine.

In the end, the process of making wine symbolizes our own personal growth and transformation. It reminds us that through embracing eternal truths and learning from those who have walked this path before us, we can transform our ego-driven desires into something truly divine - a vessel for God's love and life to flow through us without hindrance. And as we savor each sip of this "new wine," we are reminded of the journey that brought us here and the journey still to come.

Yet, Jesus' first miracle at the wedding in Cana was turning water into wine. But it's worth noting that the water was placed in six ceremonial stone jars. The number six represents humanity, as man was created on the sixth day according to biblical tradition. As we know from previous discussions on the symbolic meaning of stone, it represents stability and a foundation for truth to be established upon.

But these were not just any stone jars - they were ceremonially used for religious purposes. So, when combined, these symbols suggest that mankind has been attempting to maintain and carry the truth of God through earthly means. This is not necessarily wrong or bad, but it only reaches a certain level - represented by the water in the jars - which is limited to our literal understanding of truth.

What we truly need is new wine - a complete internal transformation and maturity that can only come from God himself rather than our own efforts. This is why Jesus is referred to as "the vine" - once his seed is planted within us, it begins to grow and expand our understanding of metaphysical truths like leaven in his parables.

No longer are we dependent on the work or teachings of others, for Christ is the true vine that produces a different kind of wine - one that is not limited by our earthly understanding or effort. This new wine represents the blissful union with God and the constant flow of his goodness through us into the world, a gift freely given without any struggle or strife.

METAPHYSICAL MEANING of WATER and BAPTISM:

Rocks, mountains, and trees stood tall and proud, each in their own designated spaces, unlike water, which flowed freely and connected everything in its path. The streams, rivers, and lakes all intertwined and merged into one giant body of water, showing the true power of interconnectedness. Water, with its natural humility, became the most dominant force on earth - the vast ocean. Just as Jesus spoke of the meek inheriting the earth, water proved that through its interconnected nature and cleansing abilities, it held the greatest power. It was not confined by physical boundaries like rocks and mountains but instead had the ability to purify and transport life in all its forms - including humanity - through its streams and rivers. In a way, water was more similar to the spiritual and psychic realm than the solid surface of our planet. It represented birth and new beginnings, as all forms of life originated from the ocean. And even within our own bodies, we began as tiny water creatures in our mother's womb, floating blissfully in the amniotic fluid. Only when we were born into this world did we take our first breath and become fully aware of our surroundings. Just like being lost at sea would disorient us without a sense of direction, so too can water symbolize chaos and instability. This duality is evident in the story of Noah's ark and the great flood - where water both cleansed and brought destruction upon mankind.

Even the most hardened sailors will tell you that the ocean is a force to be reckoned with, constantly reminding us of our own insignificance against its immense power and unpredictable nature. Its dark depths hold infinite secrets, mysteries that humans have yet to unravel and may never fully understand. Venturing into the ocean is like stepping into a whole new world, one where humans are mere visitors at the mercy of its tides and any hidden dangers lurking in the shadows. The unknown and unexplored depths of the ocean also represent our subconscious minds – a vast expanse full of life and activity but shrouded in mystery and capable of unleashing chaos when brought to the surface. In Genesis chapter 1:6, God creates a firmament to separate the waters above from the waters below. This symbolizes the division between our conscious and subconscious minds, with the latter holding infinite potential for both danger and growth. Just as clouds gather water from the ocean before raining down upon us, revealing hidden insights and truths through God's grace, so too does our subconscious bring forth thoughts and emotions that shape our lives in ways we may not fully comprehend.

As the same water drawn from the depths of the ocean now falls from the sky in gentle drops, so too does our understanding and integration of the unknown come to us in manageable pieces. This harmonizing force, referred to as Heaven in Genesis 1:6, brings balance to all things by bringing forth the dangers and mysteries of the subconscious mind, allowing them to be brought into the light of our conscious comprehension. In this way, we are able to continue on our journey of soul development.

Baptism plays a significant role in Christianity, symbolizing our death to the ego and rebirth into a new life through Christ. We are submerged in water to represent the dissolution of old mental struc-tures and thought patterns, cleansing and purifying our state of consciousness. It is like crossing over the Jordan River, leaving behind uncertainty and disorder and entering into a promised land of growth and transformation.

Our earthly attempts at baptism may take many forms, such as drowning ourselves in alcohol or immersing ourselves in rigid group ideologies. However, true spiritual baptism involves experiencing God's grace and mercy. Throughout the Bible, God is described as a consuming fire - all-powerful and intelligent with no darkness within. Eventually, anything created through our ignorant use of God's power will be burnt away by his holy love.

Through baptism, we willingly submit our egos to God's authority and receive his grace and mercy while still on earth. It is an acknowledgment of our connection to God's divine energy and a step towards deeper spiritual understanding so that on the day of the Revelation of Christ, the holy water of baptism will quench the flames of God, and we shall experience his presence as pure peace, joy and overwhelming love.

This is not a display of power from God but rather a subtle

and conscious shift within ourselves. It is a realization that everything belongs to God and comes from Him. This grace and mercy are not just concepts, but they are felt and experienced through being fully enveloped in God's love. Instead of feeling the intense heat of God's presence, we feel a cooling and peaceful love emanating from Him. Like a baby floating weightlessly in the womb, baptism allows us to let go of all guilt, shame, and baggage as we are held in the refreshing and cleansing embrace of God's grace.

As we continue on our journey of inner transformation, it is important to understand that God's grace and mercy are not simply abstract concepts or displays of power. Rather, they are experienced through a subtle and conscious shift within ourselves.

In Genesis 1:9-10, God gathers the waters under the sky into one place to reveal dry land. This symbolizes the need for us to gather all aspects of our being – both physical and spiritual – under the guidance and authority of God and present it before his alter (our hearts) in order to fully experience His grace and mercy.

When we realize that everything belongs to God and comes from Him, it becomes easier for us to submit ourselves to His will and receive His blessings. This is not about giving up our free will but rather surrendering it to the divine plan that God has in store for us.

Through this submission, we can experience a deep connection with God's love, which is described as a consuming fire in both the Old Testament (Deuteronomy 4:24) and New Testament (Hebrews 12:29). This fire represents God's all-consuming power and purity, but it can also be experienced as an overwhelming sense of love and peace once we are willing to choose, here and now to receive his grace through water, not fire.

Just as water can extinguish a physical flame, so too can the holy water of baptism quench the flames of God's presence within and all around us. Instead of feeling overwhelmed by His intense heat, we feel enveloped in His cooling and peaceful love.

As we submerge ourselves and wash away our old, rigid ways of thinking, the spirit of life brings us back to its source. We are resurrected out of the water through the fires of God, breathing in the new breath of Ruach Hakodesh (the Holy Spirit). Now, the fire no longer burns us because we have been cleansed of all impurities. Just as a newborn takes its first breath, we breathe in a new mind state that is cleansed and ready to embody the divine ideals of Christ through unity with His mind, filtered and integrated through the Holy Spirit now active in us. In this state, all aspects of life come into balance and work together harmoniously instead of causing conflict as we once experienced because all we do now is done through the will of God, which brings balance to all things as his nature is pure impartial bestowal, and so conflict ceases to exist within.

SYMBOLIC MEANING OF STONE:

Like the steady flow of blood through our veins, streams and rivers represent the lifeblood of the earth. In contrast, stones and rocks symbolize the bones of the earth, providing a solid foundation for all life to thrive upon. Their unchanging nature brings about stability, reliability, and durability - qualities that are often associated with immortality and divinity. From the earliest days of humanity, stones and rocks have held significant spiritual meaning, representing the divine force that holds all things together. Just as our bodies rely on our skeletal structure to hold us up, so too does our world rely on these ancient formations to support its existence.

The wise man builds his house upon the rock, drawing strength and security from its unwavering presence. By planting ourselves firmly upon this foundation, we are able to lay down roots and build a life filled with family, friends, and comforts. In this way, the rock becomes symbolic of faith - a sturdy base from which to grow and expand.

In the Bible, Jesus changes Simon's name to Cephas or Peter, which means "rock." This act represents the transformation of faith in one's life. Before reading and writing were common skills, knowledge was passed down through oral tradition - through hearing. By changing Simon's name from "hearing" to "rock," Jesus conveys that true understanding and an unshakable faith can be attained through hearing the word of truth.

It is important to note that Jesus never instructs us to blindly believe in something without understanding it. Instead, he encourages us to listen carefully and gain true understanding - for it is this understanding that lays the foundation for an eternal and unchanging faith.

Contrary to popular belief, Jesus never instructed us to have blind faith. He encouraged us to examine and study his word and teachings and to reach a place within ourselves where we could truly grasp and understand them. It is through this understanding that our faith is built, just like the famous story of Jacob's ladder. In this tale, the rock or stone represents faith as Jacob takes it and uses it as a pillow to rest his head upon while he sleeps. This shows us that though spiritual revelation may be obscured from our conscious mind, as long as we rest our thoughts on spiritual truths, faith will continue to grow in our subconscious until a higher spiritual realization dawns upon us.

In the story, Jacob has a vision of a ladder that connects heaven and earth, with angels representing divine ideas ascending and descending upon it. At the top stands Jehovah God, overseeing the process. This symbolizes our journey from a material understanding of faith to eventually realizing our oneness with God. When Jacob wakes up from his sleep and has this conscious realization, he proclaims, "Surely Jehovah is in this place, and I knew it not."

There's a lot more to this story, which we'll dedicate more time to later, but for now, we're only focused on the symbolism of stone.

Like a timeless legend, the tale of David and Goliath weaves together profound symbolism and spiritual meaning. Goliath stands tall and proud, adorned in the finest armor that represents the illusions of material wealth and power. Meanwhile, David, a simple shepherd boy, rejects the offered armor of King Saul and steps onto the battlefield armed with only his sling and 5 smooth stones. These smooth stones represent the refined senses, honed through the flowing waters of spiritual truth, that gives us access to a higher realm of understanding.

Goliath, the embodiment of material error thoughts devoid of spiritual life, taunts and mocks from his lofty position. But David, representing the faith in spiritual power held by the Israelites, calmly responds that God does not save with sword and spear.

With precision and faith, David slings one of his stones directly into Goliath's forehead - the seat of intellect and ego. This symbolizes the triumph of faith over the limited human mind. The stone sinks deep into Goliath's material-based thoughts, killing off his carnal mind.

This same theme is echoed in Jesus' temptation in the wilderness, where Satan tries to tempt him with food to satisfy his physical hunger. But Jesus knows that true sustenance comes from an inner relationship with God, not through satisfying earthly desires.

Ultimately, it is through this understanding and internalization of God's word that Jesus becomes the bread of life. And just as the rejected stone becomes the cornerstone in building a strong foundation, so too does our faith in God become the cornerstone of our lives.

The cornerstone, being the first stone laid in the construction of a building, holds immense symbolism and significance. It serves as the foundation upon which all other stones are perfectly aligned, ensuring the stability and strength of the entire structure. In essence, it is the very essence of perfection embodied within a material form. And for us, as believers in Christ, this cornerstone represents none other than Jesus himself.

As we delve deeper into the concept of the cornerstone, we see that it goes beyond just physical structures and buildings. In fact, it symbolizes something far greater - the perfect and unchanging foundation upon which we build our lives. Just as Apostle Paul affirms in 1 Corinthians 3:11-17, Jesus is the only true foundation that can withstand the tests and trials of life. Any other foundation will crumble under the weight of our imperfections and struggles.

But what does building on this foundational truth look like? It involves using various materials - gold, silver, jewels, wood, grass or straw - as representations of our experiences in this world. These experiences may be challenging and full of opposition, but through them, we have the opportunity to refine ourselves and bring forth higher spiritual forces into our lives.

This process is not easy - it requires sacrifice and surrendering of our own desires and ego. Yet when we offer up these experiences to God through Christ, they are transformed into something beautiful and powerful. Just as Jacob had his revelation and enlightenment with God as he wrestled with Him at Peniel (Genesis 32:22-31), so too can we have our own epiphany when we fully embrace the truth that Christ is within us always.

In this way, we become temples of God - vessels for His Spirit to reside in. And just as any disrespect or harm towards a holy temple would result in consequences from God Himself, so too must we treat ourselves with reverence and holiness.

So, let us remember the cornerstone, Christ within us. As we continue to build our lives upon His truth and sacrifice ourselves for His glory, we can rest assured that nothing can shake or destroy this perfect foundation. And in the end, when the Day of judgment comes, we will be rewarded for our faithfulness to Him. Let us hold onto this truth and let it guide us as we journey through life and towards the light of God.

THE CROSS AND THE CROWN OF THORNS:

As we delve into the significance of the cross and the crown of thorns, it is crucial to reestablish the meaning of a symbol. A symbol is not just a mere representation of something tangible but rather a convergence of multiple truths that ultimately convey a higher truth. And while some may argue that the crucifixion was merely a metaphor, as Christians, we must believe in its physical occurrence, for it is the cornerstone of our faith.

Through centuries past, everything vertical has been synonymous with divinity - poles, pillars, pyramids, and towers all serve as symbols of humanity's conscious ascension towards God. These structures seem to stretch endlessly towards the heavens, representing eternity. On the other hand, the horizontal line signifies limitation and constraint - the material world serving as a barrier for our eternal spirits.

In Christ Jesus, we see the perfect fusion of these two opposites - fully man yet fully God. As he hangs on the cross, his human form embodies the divinity of Jehovah God. The cross itself becomes a symbol of the earth, with its four cardinal points representing the four elements and seasons. And at its center hangs Christ, the 5th element that transcends beyond the cyclical nature of earthly existence. It is by surrendering our five senses to the spirit of God within us that we can break free from the limitations of this world and awaken our sixth sense or seed of our soul.

And just as Christ bore five wounds on his body - one in each hand and foot, and one in his side - let us also bear our own wounds, the purification of our carnal senses, as we nail our egos to the cross and allow God's spirit to guide us towards true understanding.

As we gaze upon the cross, we are confronted with the intersection of opposing forces. In this convergence lies a divine harmony, for at the center of these oppositions, a transcendent third element is birthed. This new creation, born from the joining of masculine and feminine energies, is made possible through the ultimate sacrifice of Jesus Christ, who united these contrasting forces in perfect balance. Through his suffering on the cross, we are granted entry into a higher dimension beyond our two-dimensional understanding. The cross thus becomes a symbol not of death but of rebirth and evolution.

At its core, the cross represents the cosmic crossroads of life, where important decisions must be made as we leave behind our past selves and embrace a new future. And yet, even as we stand at this pivotal point, time becomes fluid and all-encompassing, encompassing past, present, and future. Here stands the infinite center of existence.

This center is a place of infinite potential and possibility, for it is the dwelling place of God Himself - the unknowable Absolute before all manifestation. And yet, through His Word - Christ - He reveals Himself to us and allows us to know Him through the limitations of our finite understanding. Just as Mary was found with a child from the Holy Spirit - the living substance that permeates all creation - so too do we carry within us the potential for divine creation.

In surrendering to these universal laws and embracing our limitations, we find true immortality and eternal life. For just as Jesus opened up the way to eternity at the crossroads where opposites converge, so too do our own paths lead to everlasting glory when we unite with God through His divine plan.

The center, circle, or circumference represents infinity, as the circle has no beginning and no end. "But you, O Lord, reign forever; your throne endures to all generations." (Lamentations 5:19) God the Absolute, Elohim, is ultimately unknowable because he's before all manifestation. "Great is our Lord, and abundant in power; his understanding is beyond measure." (Psalm 147:5) However, in the beginning was the word and the word was with God and was God, this word is Christ, Logos, which is the wisdom of God, from and through which all things generate and through this generation God can become known. But Christ is the stream of divine intelligence that knows no limit, and so a limitation needs to be placed upon Christ in order for manifestation to take place. This limitation, on a macrocosmic scale, is what we could refer to as the womb of creation, the Holy Spirit, and on the microcosmic scale, it's the womb of Mary. It's the living substance that permeates all creation. This is the Holy Spirit, or whole/undivided spirit of God, and why Mary was found to be with child from the Holy Spirit. "The angel answered her, 'The Holy Spirit will come upon you, and the power of the Most High will overshadow you; therefore the child to be born will be called holy—the Son of God.'" (Luke 1:35) It's the place where the divine ideals of Christ gestate, get turned over, and developed into something that is tangible. In order for them to be tangible and therefore known to all creation, limitation or restriction must be initiated and maintained. This balance of infinity with limitation is revealed to us in the image of the cross. Jesus on the cross, is showing us that the way of eternity is opened at the convergence of opposites, and that we must surrender to the laws of the universe, which at first makes us seem like a victim, but in reality, this surrender becomes our immortality. "And whoever does not take his cross and follow me is not worthy of me." (Matthew 10:38)

In John 19:17 we are told this all takes place in Golgotha, which is Hebrew for the place of the skull. This circumference at the center of the cross we are talking about is related to our human head, or the place of the scull. The rose bush is both a symbol of pleasure and pain, of the beauty of life (the flower) along with the certainty of death that comes with it (the thorn). And so the rose bush with flower, and thorn, life and death, infinity and limitation embodies the same meanings as the cross. Notice first that the thorn stem comes first then the rose bud opens up, the suffering of our carnal body is the stem that rises toward the sun and acts as a pillar for the beauty of our soul body to unfold. This is the same meaning as "first in the natural, then in the spiritual," as the Apostle Paul tells us. "For as by a man came death, by a man has come also the resurrection of the dead. For as in Adam all die, so also in Christ all shall live."

THE CUBE, THE CROSS AND THE THRONE:

The symbol of a cornerstone has deep biblical roots and is often used as a metaphor for Jesus Christ. In this chapter, we will explore the significance of the cornerstone, which is the shape of a cube and its connection to the life and teachings of Jesus.

A cornerstone is the first stone laid in place when building a structure, and it serves as the foundation upon which the rest of the building is constructed. It is precisely measured and aligned to determine the positioning of all other stones in the construction. The quality and strength of a cornerstone determine the stability and durability of the entire building.

In biblical references, Jesus is often referred to as the cornerstone or foundation stone. In Psalm 118:22, it says, "the stone which the builders rejected has become the chief cornerstone." This verse was later referenced by Jesus in Matthew 21:42, where he identified himself as this rejected stone that would become the most important part of God's plan.

When we look at Jesus' life and teachings, we can see how he fulfilled this role as a cornerstone. He came into a world that rejected him, yet through his death and resurrection, he became the unshakable foundation of our faith. He is our rock on which we build everything else in our lives.

Just like a physical cornerstone must be precisely measured and aligned for a building to stand strong, Jesus provides us with a moral compass and divine ideals by which we can align our lives. His teachings serve as guidelines for living a fulfilling and righteous life.

The cube shape, with all sides perfectly equal, is often used to represent this cornerstone or foundation stone. It also holds significance in its meaning as a 3-dimensional square, representing stability, harmony, unity, and truth, for it is unchanging and unmoving. The number four is associated with the cube because each side is square, and just as the number four represents nature because of the four elements - four directions, four seasons, and four phases of the moon, it is intrinsically connected to the meaning of the cube.

In the Bible, the number seven is often associated with completeness and perfection. In fact, the creation story in Genesis speaks of God creating the world in six days and resting on the seventh day, signifying completion and rest.

The cube shape also holds this significance of completeness, with its six sides representing all directions - north, south, east, west, up, and down. The central point represents God's presence and sovereignty over all.

This symbolism is further reinforced when we look at the concept of the sevenfold spirit of God. In Isaiah 11:2, it says, "the Spirit of the Lord shall rest upon him [the Messiah], the Spirit of wisdom and understanding, the Spirit of counsel and might, the Spirit of knowledge and the fear of the Lord." This verse speaks of seven distinct attributes or characteristics of God's spirit that are present in Jesus.

These seven spirits can also be seen as representing different aspects or functions of God's nature - wisdom for guidance and discernment, understanding for empathy and compassion, counsel for wise decision making, might for strength and power, knowledge for truth and insight, fear of the Lord for reverence and respect.

When we combine these seven spirits together with their representation in a cube shape with its central point symbolizing God's presence, we get a powerful image. It portrays a complete understanding and embodiment of who God is - a sovereign being with infinite wisdom, love, power, justice, mercy and holiness.

It's interesting to note that if we place a hexagram, also known as the Seal of Solomon or Star of David, within a hexagon - a six-sided shape - we can create converging lines that lead us to the center point. By connecting these lines, we transform this two-dimensional shape into a three-dimensional cube. This cube represents our multi-dimensional universe, held together by seven elements. The seventh point, residing in the center of the cube, represents the I AM consciousness because of its unmoving, unchanging presence. Each side of the cube has its own dynamic direction, with each direction opposing its counterpart. Up and down, left and right, forward and back, yet the central seventh point remains still and unchanging amidst all this movement. It is because of this that the number seven is considered holy, and why God rested on the seventh day after creating the universe through six stages. Just as the cube has six sides balanced by a seventh element at its center, so too does our universe revolve around this sacred number seven - as seen in the creation story in Genesis 1.

Because of this, it's simple logic to conclude that there is a 7th dimension within which this 3-dimensional realm, the cube, is held together. Since time and space can only exist in the realm of three dimensions, we can also conclude that the 7th dimension, which is the 7th point in the cube, is beyond time and space and so eternal. This is what we refer to as the spiritual realm or Kingdom of Heaven. It's the realm of divine ideals which, through the synthesis of their elemental forms crystalize into the material realm. Once again, this is why the number 7 is so prevalent all throughout the bible and what the number 7 represents in Revelation is the cleansing and regenerating of each of these dimensions.

By understanding this concept, we can also gain insight into the biblical meaning behind numbers like 5, 10, and 12. In our 3-dimensional universe, there are 6 directions: forward, back, left, right, up, and down. When the 4th dimension of spacetime is added, it creates a continuum that encompasses past and future, similar to how God exists beyond time and space. And at the core of all this lies our "I Am" presence or spirit.

If we were to unfold the cube, it would reveal a cross with its center being the bottom square of the cube. This is reminiscent of Jesus Christ's crucifixion on a cross made from unfolding a cube. Just as his body was opened up on the cross with blood and water, baptizing the earth and flowing out when his side was pierced, so too does the unfolded cube reveal a central point representing higher dimensions of spirit that keep our universe in balance.

The shape of the cross itself represents the 4 cardinal points - north, east, south, and west - but with the addition of a fifth element: Jesus' body. As he represents the embodiment of spiritual principles in a microcosmic way, so too do our five senses play a role in unifying us with God's will. This is symbolized by the five wounds of Christ - one for each point in our human body: head, arms (left and right), and legs (left and right). Through these wounds, Christ solidifies the connection between our spiritual and physical existence. Without making this selfless sacrifice, trying to understand divine principles while still stuck in our superficial selves would have serious consequences. However, Jesus was without sin and therefore not bound by karmic ties, allowing us to embody his nature and adopt his mindset, transforming our inner being into a state of Christ-like enlightenment without any negative repercussions. This is possible because the blood of Christ and the sacrifice he made for us were pure and just, rendering us immune to any attacks from evil forces. "We know [with confidence] that anyone born of God does not habitually sin, but He (Jesus) who was born of God [carefully] keeps and protects him, and the evil one does not touch him." - 1 John 5:18.

As we have discussed before, the center of the cross represents its circumference - much like the center of our heads or skulls. This promise leads to a new crown - one of eternal life - if we absorb the revelation of Christ's sacrifice and align ourselves with his heart at its center. Through this alignment, we can enter into a new reality of life in higher dimensions with Jesus as our guide.

As the cube, the embodiment of this 3-dimensional universe, is carefully unfolded and its hidden center is revealed to be the spirit of God in man, embodied by Jesus Christ on the cross, a sense of awe and reverence fills the air. The sheer weight of this revelation presses down upon those who witness it, as the stone that seals the tomb must now be closed once again to restore balance. Yet with this knowledge of the mystery of mysteries, the stone can be removed at will by the hands of Christ, allowing for a deeper under-standing and connection to the divine.

Like a puzzle coming together, the cube is folded back up and becomes a throne upon which Jesus and his followers will sit beyond the constraints of time and space at the very heart of all creation. Through our union with Christ and his sacrifice, we have transcended psychological death and are no longer bound by the impermanence of this world. We now operate from our divine nature, sitting upon the unwavering principles of God.

The base of Solomon's throne, described in 1 Kings, consisted of six steps leading up to a central seventh point - representing the process we must undergo to reach our eternal seat upon the throne. Just as the legs of the throne rise out of the chaos of earth or primordial consciousness up toward heaven, so too do we rise from earthly concerns towards divine consciousness, anchored in the true reality of being. Those who have experienced the sacrifice of Jesus inwardly will sit upon this cube of three-dimensional space and time and know no death, for they have become one with Christ, their true self. To them, all forms of life and death are mere fleeting stages, while their identity in Christ remains constant and unchanging.

SYMBOLIC MEANING OF THE WELL:

Throughout the pages of the Bible, the symbol of the well can be found repeatedly. From Abraham and his son Isaac digging and protecting seven wells, to Moses driving away aggressors at a well in Exodus, to Jesus revealing himself as the well of living water at Jacob's well in John 4:7. This recurring theme of wells, particularly associated with the number seven, is directly linked to the seven seals and the lamb in the book of Revelation - a tantalizing glimpse of what is yet to come.

But why are these wells so prevalent in the bible? And what significance does the number seven hold in this context? To fully understand their spiritual meaning, we must consider their relationship to everything around them and how they are experienced within our consciousness.

These wells were often located in the desert, a harsh and arid environment. The dryness of the desert is antithetical to organic life, which thrives in moist environments with a balance of darkness and light. Yet hidden underneath the barren landscape, these wells act as channels for life-giving water. There is a stark contrast between the dry heat of the desert above and the cool darkness beneath where water flows. By learning to tap into this source, we can transform desolation into abundance and create new life where there was once only death.

However, it is important to note that the desert and its dryness are also symbolic of an overabundance of fire - representing passion and zeal. It is in this place of extreme heat and barrenness that we have the opportunity to burn away material and emotional baggage and reconnect with God's eternal presence. This is demonstrated by biblical figures such as Moses, Elijah, and Jesus, who all spent time in the desert to purify themselves spiritually.

But just as these wells bring forth new life from what was once deemed dead, so too can we transform ourselves through the trials and challenges of our own inner deserts. Like a desert flower blooming amidst harsh conditions, we, too, have the potential for growth and renewal when we tap into the life-giving waters within us. The symbolism of wells and their association with the number seven further emphasizes this idea of transformation and rebirth, as we are reminded to continually strive towards spiritual growth and a closer connection with God.

The purpose of incarnation is a daunting task, a bridge that must span the vast expanse of opposing forces. It requires finding a delicate balance between remaining in the light of God and being sustained enough emotionally and materially to expand and grow, synchronizing all elements of life into a cohesive whole.

In the harsh, barren desert landscape, there lies an undercurrent of water hidden deep below the surface. This precious resource can only be found by those who know how to look for it. But once located, the real work begins: digging, establishing structures and containers, lowering them down into the cold and dark depths of the earth to pull up the refreshing waters. This act symbolizes bridging the gap from an unknown and subversive underworld to the light of comprehension on the surface.

Peering down into a well evokes a sense of mystery and wonder as if gazing into another realm. The darkness and dampness are countered by a shimmering pool of water at the bottom, reminiscent of a hidden network of life pulsing like veins beneath the earth's surface. The well also holds symbolism for the feminine principle; its dark tunnel leading to life-giving waters mirrors the journey through a vagina to reach the womb, where new life is developed and sustained.

It is no coincidence that wells hold significant meaning in religious texts. In John 4:14, Jesus speaks about the free gift of eternal life represented by water from a well: "Whoever drinks the water I give them will never thirst. Indeed, the water I give them will become in them a spring of water welling up to eternal life."

Here, Christ represents the hidden source within our souls, waiting for us to lower our vessels and draw out this life-giving essence. This is where the number 7 becomes intertwined with the symbolism of the well – representing completeness and perfection in accessing this divine source within ourselves.

The LAMB of GOD:

The lamb symbolizes purity, innocence, and optimistic joy. It is born in the spring, a season of new beginnings and life after the cold and dark winter. So, what does it mean that Jesus is referred to as the lamb slain before the world's creation? And why is he the only one worthy enough to open the seven seals in Revelation?

In this corrupt world, we are all born innocent but cannot remain so for long. We must develop a tough exterior to protect ourselves from harm, physical or mental. This leads to building our ego and our personal self, which goes against the nature of God - selfless and all-encompassing.

To become one with God, we must first become nothing. As long as we are confined within our limited selves, we cannot experience the eternal peace and power of God. Therefore, we must cast away Satan - represented by our false sense of self - in order to fully unite with God. This is achieved through "the blood of the Lamb" and bearing witness to our faith even unto death.

The Lamb of God represents a purified and humble ego that allows for God's manifestation through it, just as Jesus demonstrated as the ego-consciousness of Christ. This is why he is known as the Lamb of God.

No ego-driven individual has the authority to open the seven seals mentioned in Revelation 5. These seals represent our current stage of psycho-spiritual development - each one of us being a book with written information about ourselves on both sides. It signifies all the experiences and memories stored within us and those left behind in our wake.

The heavy weight of the seven seals looms over us, presenting a formidable barrier that must be conquered in order to attain the next stage of our psycho-spiritual evolution. Throughout history, these same seals have halted the progress of every individual who has strived to become One with God. Despite this, there was one who understood the necessary process to reach such a heightened state of consciousness. Ironically, he showed us that it can only be achieved through the complete opposite means of what humanity had previously believed. To merge with the Ancient of Days, we must strip ourselves down to the most pure and vulnerable form - like a lamb among wolves. By embodying this innocent and harmless nature, as exemplified by Jesus, we gain access to the power of the lamb and are granted the privilege of being fully united with God.

Just as Jesus Christ serves as an example on a grand scale, when we take up his cause, this transformation begins within us on a smaller scale. This is the true meaning behind the book of Revelation, which we will delve into more deeply in the near future. For now, it is crucial to understand that humbling our ego and personal self holds the same significance as picking up our cross and dying to ourselves each day. Once our ego is slain, we are resurrected as the mighty Lion of Judah - the spirit of Christ within us. As Paul writes in Galatians 2:20, "I have been crucified with Christ [in Him I have shared His crucifixion]; it is no longer I who live, but Christ lives in me."

In the person of Jesus Christ, two natures are fully personified - that of the lamb and the lion. The humble ego and the divine Christ. Throughout all of human history, the lion has been synonymous with the sun - a symbol of strength, power, and vitality. Its golden color and thick, majestic mane spread out like rays of sunlight from its face. The name Judah means "praise," and through humbling ourselves and turning away from selfish desires, we display to God our readiness for His Almighty power to fill us. This is represented by the lion, or solar force, which brings light, knowledge, and life. It is through this Lion of Judah, or the Christic solar force of Praise that we gain the right to open the seven seals of the scroll. And it is the sacrificial Lamb of God who carries out this act of opening, as He has become the vessel through which God's will is carried out.

Revelation 5:6 tells us that this slain Lamb has seven eyes and seven horns. According to Saint John in Revelation, these seven eyes represent the seven spirits of God sent out into all the world. In Matthew 6:22, Jesus himself explains that the eye is like a lamp for the body - it looks outward and inward, serving as a window for the spirit within. To truly see something or someone is to perceive and understand something inwardly.

The concept of sight is often associated with physical light, but even if the sun and moon were to disappear at this very moment, our consciousness would still enable us to perceive life. As stated in John 1:4, "In him was life, and that life was the light of all mankind." Our true sight does not come from the eyes but from our consciousness. Just as Justice, symbolized by blind eyes, is able to see the truth. This is further supported by Revelation 21, which describes the New Jerusalem as a cube with six sides, representing the six directions of our three-dimensional reality. However, the center of this cube represents a higher dimension where all six directions converge. The Lamb having seven eyes signifies its spiritual perception into every aspect of our lives and its ability to unlock the obstacles preventing our spiritual growth through the opening of the seven seals.

These physical directions hold great psychological and spiritual significance as they form the basis of who we are. We are constantly moving forward in life, for stagnation leads to regression. With each step we take, we leave behind a past and strive towards a better version of ourselves, aspiring to higher levels of being. Yet, despite these efforts, we all experience highs and lows in life. These external and internal fluctuations are mirrored by the rising and setting of the sun; its ascent in the east represents the dawn of spiritual enlightenment and, therefore hope where we can connect with the world and progress, our outward expression and interactions with the world, while its descent in the west symbolizes the closing of our work and a return to our hidden inner state which may be unknown to others. However, all of this takes place within our consciousness - an unchanging entity represented by Jehovah God, or I Am - which serves as the eternal center around which our lives revolve.

Horns grow out of the top of the head, the center of the intellect, as an extension of the earth, and so represent the will that serves only the self in an aggressive, dominating manner. This is typified in the image of two goats ramming their heads together to assert dominance. It represents an adverse state of mind.

This idea is illustrated through the imagery of two goats butting heads in a display of dominance. In Judaism, the shofar, made from a ram's horn, is blown as a call to repentance and humility, as breath represents the spirit. This symbolizes our ego dying and being replaced by a humble spirit, allowing us to channel God's will. Spirit is synonymous with the breath, and so when the ram's horn is blown through, it comes to represent the very same thing that the Lamb of God represents, which is the humbled ego, the ego that has learned its role as the channel through which the spirit of God, or breath, can flow through to create change upon the material world through a higher vibration.

According to scripture, the Lamb of God has seven horns, representing its ability to carry out God's will in all aspects of our lives. Once this slain Lamb, with seven eyes and seven horns, is at the center of our being, along with the Lion of Judah and the throne of God, then the Lamb will begin to break the seven seals that are keeping locked the Book of our lives and in so doing we will be able to consciously evolve to the level of Christ. This is the true and real Revelation of Jesus Christ.

<u>METAPHYSICAL MEANING of INSCENCE</u>:

As the Magi knelt before the newborn Messiah, they presented their offerings of Frankincense and Myrrh. These precious gifts used ceremonially for thousands of years, held deep significance in both physical and metaphysical realms.

Frankincense symbolized royalty, a fitting tribute to the infant who would become king. In ancient times, it was considered more valuable than gold and was reserved for use in religious ceremonies.

It was burned as incense to honor deities and symbolized divinity and purity.

In this context, Frankincense represents our own divine nature and our connection to God. Just as the Magi offered it to Jesus as an acknowledgment of his special divine status, we can also use it to honor and strengthen our own spiritual connection. As we burn Frankincense, its sweet aroma fills the air and reminds us of the presence of divinity within us.

Myrrh, with its bitter scent, represented death, cleansing, and mourning. Like Frankincense, it was also derived from tree sap - the lifeblood of nature - making it a pure form of earth. In Judaism and ancient Egyptian cultures, Myrrh was used in purification rituals and as an embalming agent for deceased bodies.

Metaphysically, Myrrh represents transformation and rebirth. Its bitter scent symbolizes the process of shedding old ways and beliefs that no longer serve us in order to make room for new growth. This is reflected in its traditional use during funerals - a time when we must let go of a physical body in order for the soul to continue on its journey.

Together with Frankincense, Myrrh represents both life and death - two aspects that are intertwined in our existence. As we journey through life, we experience both joyous celebrations (represented by Frankincense) and moments of grief (represented by Myrrh). These two gifts remind us that both are necessary for our growth and evolution.

However, it was not just the symbolic meanings that made these gifts perfect for spiritual rituals. The solid, condensed earth held within itself a mysterious power - one that could transform into ethereal smoke when set aflame. This fragrant smoke, spiraling upwards towards the heavens, was believed to be a pleasing offering to God. As Psalm 141 states, "Let my prayer be set forth before thee as incense; and the lifting up of my hands as the evening sacrifice."

As the incense burned, its sweet aroma filled the air and permeated the atmosphere. It served as a powerful symbol for transformation within ourselves - just as the flame ignited the resin, an initial revelation or moment of enlightenment can ignite our consciousness. And like the finer ash left behind by the incense, over time, this heat burns away our limiting beliefs and false ideologies, purifying us.

Through this act of surrendering our earthly desires and limitations to God's omnipresence, omniscience, and omnipotence, we are transmuting them into a higher spiritual energy. As David prayed in Psalm 141, let our prayers be like incense and our lifted hands be seen as a sacrifice - for by honoring God in this way, we are elevating ourselves closer to Him through the transformative power of fire and smoke.

METAPHYSICAL MEANING of the FOOT and the SANDAL:

Our feet, the furthest extremities from our heads and the centers of our intelligence, serve as our connection to the earth and keep us grounded in reality. They are the natural rulers of space and time, guiding us on our path toward progress. In biblical references, our feet symbolize understanding. In Joshua 1:3, God promises Joshua that every place he sets his foot upon will be given to him. This means that whatever we can grasp and comprehend in life, we have the ability to conquer and master. Our experiences in life are shaped by where we stand and how we see the world around us. To truly understand something, we must make direct contact with it, allowing ourselves to fully experience it and gain a deeper understanding.

In John 13, Jesus humbly washes the feet of his disciples. In ancient times, it was customary for servants or disciples to wash their masters' feet, but Jesus turned this tradition on its head. To our limited human minds, this act may seem backward, but in a spiritual sense, we can understand that Christ is the embodiment of God's selflessness and pure giving. As stated in Matthew 23:11, "The greatest among you shall be your servant." By washing his disciples' feet, Jesus symbolically cleanses their false understandings of the world and removes any psychological hindrances so they can follow in his footsteps and gain a deeper spiritual understanding.

The sandal, or shoe, holds a deeper symbolic meaning as a protective barrier between us and the realm of reality. The sole of our foot, being highly sensitive, is shielded by this layer to allow us to venture into unknown terrain and gain new experiences. However, it also serves as a way to insulate and numb us from uncomfortable or painful experiences, hindering our soul growth. This covering can be seen as a representation of our preconceived notions, prejudices, and beliefs formed from past experiences.

Shoes, or sandals, have become an important aspect of fashion in many cultures. They are not just functional items to protect our feet but also a way to express our style and status. From designer brands to flashy heels, shoes have become a symbol of wealth and status, showcasing our material possessions and separating us from others.

In biblical times, shoes were also seen as a symbol of wealth and social status. In the story of the prodigal son in Luke 15:22, the father orders that his son be given sandals as a sign of his restored position as part of the family. The wealthy in ancient times would often wear ornate sandals with jewels or gold embellishments.

But beyond mere material possessions, shoes also represent our egos – the sense of self-worth and identity that we project to the world. Just as we carefully choose our shoes to reflect our personality and social standing, we also construct personas for ourselves based on our past experiences and societal expectations.

For example, someone who has experienced rejection or trauma may adopt an aloof or guarded personality to protect themselves from being hurt again. Similarly, someone who is praised and rewarded for their accomplishments may develop an inflated ego and feel superior to others.

Our egos can serve as barriers between ourselves and God. It is easy to get caught up in worldly pursuits and become disconnected from our spiritual nature. We put on different masks to fit in with society or maintain a certain image, which can prevent us from truly connecting with God.

This is why the act of removing one's sandals holds such significance in many religions and spiritual practices. In Hinduism and Buddhism, it is customary to remove one's shoes before entering a temple or sacred space to show respect and humility towards higher powers.

In Judaism, God instructed Moses to remove his sandals before approaching Him at the burning bush (Exodus 3:5). This act symbolizes removing our protective layers and exposing ourselves to God's inspirations.

ON HEAVEN:

Heaven is not a physical place but rather a state of being that aligns with the thoughts and ideals of God. It exists everywhere and manifests in our minds, bodies, and lives as an orderly and harmonious expression of God's kingdom. According to Jesus, heaven is within us - the place where the divine ideas of God are fully realized. On Earth, we are tasked with bringing these ideals into physical existence through time and space. This process is often represented through parables, such as the growth of a mustard seed or the expansion of leaven in bread, which we have gone over in the section of this book discussing the kingdom parables in the book of Matthew. As we ascend in consciousness and reach a singularity point, we will experience the full revelation of Jesus Christ, which is depicted in the book of Revelation. From this point on, we will dwell within the cube - the new Jerusalem or fully redeemed 3-dimensional realm that perfectly represents our physical universe. At the center of this cube will be God himself, eternally enthroned in our hearts. And alongside him will be the Lamb of God - our humbled and purified ego - who will enact his will. This is the ultimate purpose of all creation - for humanity to humble itself and come back to God as vessels for his divine purposes, as exemplified by the life of Jesus of Nazareth. By becoming the lowest, we become the highest form of creation in God's eyes. Believe it or not, this is the original claim of Christianity, and it is not so hard to realize if the whole purpose of being a Christian is to follow Christ.

God longs for us to become fully immersed in His divine nature, to be one with Him as we were originally created. This truth was the foundation of early Christianity, but over time, it has been distorted by society and even within the Church itself. However, Jesus himself acknowledged this truth when he said, "The kingdom of God is within you" (Luke 17:21). This kingdom refers to the state of being where God's divine nature is fully realized and expressed. In other words, heaven is within us, waiting to be uncovered.

When we align our thoughts, actions, and intentions with God's will and purpose, we become channels for His divine love and power. Our inner Christ - the part of us that is made in the image and likeness of God - becomes fully awakened. This is not an external figure or deity that we worship but rather a state of consciousness that we embody.

The early Christian mystics understood this oneness with God through their practice of contemplative prayer and meditation. They sought to silence their ego-driven thoughts and connect directly with God's spirit within them. They believed that this was the only way to truly know God and experience a deep union with Him.

However, over time, these mystical practices were replaced by rigid doctrines and rules within the Church. The focus shifted from inner transformation to outer conformity. As a result, many Christians today have lost touch with their inner Christ and are more concerned with following external rules rather than finding true oneness with God.

But Jesus came not to establish a new religion or set of rules but to awaken us to our innate divinity and help us realize our true purpose - to become one with God. He showed us through his own life how humbling oneself before God leads to exaltation in His eyes.

As we align ourselves with the teachings of Jesus and seek an intimate relationship with Him through prayer and meditation, we can awaken the Christ within us and experience the fullness of God in us.

The belief in our deification through Christ's incarnation is a core tenet of Christian theology. This idea is based on the understanding that Jesus, as the Son of God, took on human flesh in order to redeem and deify humanity. This concept is expressed in John 1:14, "And the Word became flesh and lived among us, and we have seen his glory, the glory as of a father's only son, full of grace and truth." This means that through Jesus' incarnation, we are able to partake in God's divine nature and become more like Him.

Athanasius, a fourth-century Bishop of Alexandria, wrote extensively on this topic in his work On the Incarnation. He emphasized that Jesus' incarnation was necessary for our salvation and deification. Athanasius believed that because humanity had fallen from its original state of communion with God through sin, it needed to be restored back to its original state. And this could only be achieved by God himself taking on human form.

Through His incarnation, Jesus not only showed us how to live a holy life but also made it possible for us to participate in His divine nature. As Athanasius wrote, "He was made human so that he might make us gods." This statement highlights the belief that our destiny as Christians is to be fully deified and inherit eternal life.

This belief is also reflected in various scriptures throughout the Bible. In Psalm 82:6, it says, "I said, 'You are gods; you are all sons of the Most High.'" Here, God is speaking to earthly rulers but also hinting at our potential for deification through our connection with Him. Similarly, Jesus quotes this verse in John 10:34 when defending his divinity against accusations from Jewish religious leaders.

Additionally, the New Testament writers also speak about our participation in God's divine nature through Christ. In 2 Peter 1:4, it says, "By these he has given us his very great and precious promises, so that through them you may participate in the divine nature, having escaped the corruption in the world caused by evil desires." The Apostle Paul writes in Romans 8:19, "For [even the whole] creation (all nature) waits expectantly and longs earnestly for God's sons to be made known [waits for the revealing, the disclosing of their sonship]." This means that once we, humanity, awaken to the fact that we are truly conduits for the presence of God to experience his creation through us, all the earth will be in turmoil because the inner state of humanity is in turmoil. Once we become the manifest body of Christ, all the earth will join us in its deification. As Isaiah writes in Isaiah 11:6, "The wolf also shall dwell with the lamb, The leopard shall lie down with the young goat, The calf and the young lion and the fatling together; And a little child shall lead them." The child shall lead them because, as Christ said, unless you are a child (egoless, innocent and trusting in God), you will not see the kingdom of God.

However, this concept can be dangerous if approached with an egotistical mindset. The ego must die in order for our true deification to take place, just as Jesus surrendered his own life on the cross. We must become nothing in order to truly become God. For God is all-encompassing and without ego. Therefore, our claim to godhood cannot come from a place of pride or self-importance. It is only through humility and surrender that we can fully embody the divinity within us and be a vessel for God's will to manifest in this world. As Jesus taught us, "Whoever tries to hold onto their life will lose it, but whoever loses their life for my sake will find it" (Matthew 16:25). Let us strive to become like Christ, emptying ourselves of our own desires and allowing God's love and light to flow through us completely.

In Conclusion

My friends, my hope in writing this book is that you will continue to fight the good fight. "I have told you these things, so that in me you may have peace. In this world you will have trouble. But take heart! I have overcome the world." (John 16:33). As Jesus teaches in the Lord's Prayer, "Our Father who is in Heaven, hallowed be your name. Your kingdom come, you will be done, on earth as it is in Heaven." In Luke 17:20-21, Jesus says, "The kingdom of God does not come with observation; nor will they say, 'Look here!' or 'Look there!' For indeed, the kingdom of God is within you."

Thus, when He says, "Our Father in Heaven," He is directing our attention inward, then declares, "Let your kingdom come, and you will be done." This signifies that God's will is not manifested in our lives unless we invoke it with reverence for the Holy Father's will to be done, acknowledging its supreme righteousness. Hence, the necessity of daily prayer. Within each of us lies a dormant spiritual being that needs to be awakened and nourished daily with the bread of life, the Word of God, enabling us to live from the inside out, not in a hypnotic trance induced by the world's distractions.

Deep within each of us lies a sacred place where Christ always presides over mass. We are all invited to enter this space and sit with our brothers and sisters, basking in the warm glow of Christ's love. I have personally experienced this love, and it set my heart ablaze. It was as if my heart would burst from the intensity of his love. This is the powerful love of Christ that can conquer any evil. It is an unshakable kingdom, impenetrable by thieves or antichrists who try to deceive with their false teachings.

But antichrists will always try, especially with the rise of social media bringing forward countless "gurus" and "spiritual masters." The true sign of spiritual enlightenment is being able to recognize that Christ Jesus was the greatest of all spiritual masters. The mere image of him, a man without sin, dying on the cross while proclaiming to save us from our own sins, is the ultimate test to see if one is truly ready to awaken spiritually. Take some time to reflect on the crucifixion of Christ and consider why he did it; pay attention to your emotions during this introspection because they will reveal where you stand spiritually.

That is the genius of Christ's teachings. If a teacher claims to teach the same principles without acknowledging Christ, they are deceiving their followers. These teachers are more focused on gaining a large following and avoiding controversy by refusing to mention Jesus Christ, the most controversial and polarizing figure in history. This proves they are simply driven by ego and financial gain, as having more followers means more money. Therefore, anyone who does not acknowledge Jesus in their new age teachings can be considered anti-Christ.

Keep the word of God in your heart always, meditating on it day and night because, as I've stated, the whole reason for this three-dimensional world of dense physicality is to grow our spiritual, immortal body. The Bible is the road map of humanity's conscious evolution, from infantile to fully ripened and ready to fall off the tree and spread its seeds. This is why the book of Revelation is the final book of the bible because it is the symbolic canon of what we each individually go through when we receive Christ into our hears, "the quickening spirit," who goes to work waking, testing and refining our inner spiritual being, or soul body. This whole game of life doesn't get any clearer than when Christ tells the Apostle John in Revelation 3:21, To him that overcometh, will I grant to sit with Me on My throne, even as I also overcame and am set down with My Father on His throne.

Leave all your limiting thoughts, ideas and beliefs in the tomb of materiality and resurrect with Jesus into the dawn of a new and eternal day, where you will no longer oscillate from light times and dark times, as spoken of in Revelation 22:5, "There will be no more night. They will not need the light of a lamp or the light of the sun, for the Lord God will give them light. And they will reign forever and ever."

I'll finally end with a quote from the English philosopher Francis Bacon, "The knowledge of man is as the waters, some descending from above, and some springing up from beneath; the one informed by the light of nature, the other inspired by divine revelation." Remember Jesus at Jacobs Well with the Samaritan women. What did he say to her? "The one who believes in me, as the Scripture has said, will have streams of living water flow from deep within him." Jesus tore a hole in the fabric of our race-thought and provided us with a ladder with which to climb up and out (his cross). We can now declare with boldness and confidence that we are the offspring of God, his perfect image and likeness and One spirit with him, dead to the world and alive forever more.

SCRIPTURES TO MEDITATE ON:

Lastly, I'll leave you with some of my favorite scriptures to declare over yourself and meditate on that I've used to help transform my inner self,

I have the mind of Christ (1 Corinthians 2:16; Philippians 2:5).

I am free forever from condemnation. (Romans 8:1).

I am alive with Christ (Ephesians 2:5).

I have the peace of God that surpasses all understanding (Philippians 4:7).

I am free from the law of sin and death (Romans 8:2).

I am born of God, and the evil one does not touch me (1 John 5:18).

I have received the power of the Holy Spirit and He can do miraculous things through me. I have authority and power over the enemy in this world (Mark 16:17-18; Luke 10:17-19).

I am the light of the world (Matthew 5:14).

You are dead to sin and alive in Christ Jesus. (Romans 6:11)

I am a temple of God, his Holy Spirit dwells in me. (1 Corinthians 3:16)